# 1,000 AMAZING RECORD BREAKERS

**THIRD EDITION**
**DK Delhi**
**Assistant art editor** Diya Varma
**Senior picture researcher** Sumedha Chopra
**Senior art editor** Vikas Chauhan
**Managing art editor** Govind Mittal
**Production editor** Jaypal Singh Chauhan
**Jacket designer** Juhi Sheth
**DTP designers** Pawan Kumar
**DTP coordinator** Vishal Bhatia
**Senior jackets coordinator** Priyanka Sharma Saddic

**DK London**
**Senior editor** Ian Fitzgerald
**Project art editor** Mary Sandberg
**Managing editor** Rachel Fox
**US senior editor** Jennette ElNaggar
**Managing art editor** Owen Peyton Jones
**Production controller** Joss Moore
**Jacket designer** Akiko Kato
**Jacket design development manager** Sophia MTT
**Publisher** Andrew Macintyre
**Associate publishing director** Liz Wheeler
**Art director** Karen Self
**Publishing director** Jonathan Metcalf

**Contributor** Andrea Mills

Content previously published in *Record Breakers!*

**FIRST EDITION**
**Senior editor** Rob Houston
**Editors** Helen Abramson, Wendy Horobin, Steve Setford, Rona Skene
**Designers** David Ball, Peter Laws, Clare Marshall, Anis Sayyed, Jemma Westing
**Illustrators** Adam Benton, Stuart Jackson-Carter, Anders Kjellberg, Simon Mumford
**Creative retouching** Steve Willis
**Picture research** Martin Copeland, Aditya Katyal
**Jacket design** Jessica Bentall, Laura Brim, Jemma Westing
**Jacket editor** Manisha Majithia
**Jacket design development manager** Sophia M Tampakopoulos Turner
**Producer (pre-production)** Rebekah Parsons-King
**Production controller** Mandy Inness
**Managing art editor** Philip Letsu
**Managing editor** Gareth Jones
**Publisher** Andrew Macintyre
**Art director** Phil Ormerod
**Associate publishing director** Liz Wheeler
**Publishing director** Jonathan Metcalf

**Author** Andrea Mills

This American Edition, 2024
First American Edition, 2018
Published in the United States by DK Publishing
a division of Penguin Random House LLC
1745 Broadway, 20th Floor, New York, NY 10019

Copyright © 2018, 2024 Dorling Kindersley Limited
24 25 26 27 28 10 9 8 7 6 5 4 3
003–339257–Aug/2024

All rights reserved.
Without limiting the rights under the copyright reserved above, no part of this publication may be reproduced, stored in or introduced into a retrieval system, or transmitted, in any form, or by any means (electronic, mechanical, photocopying, recording, or otherwise), without the prior written permission of the copyright owner.
Published in Great Britain by Dorling Kindersley Limited

A catalog record for this book is available
from the Library of Congress.
ISBN 978-0-7440-9880-8
Printed and bound in Malaysia

www.dk.com

This book was made with Forest Stewardship Council™ certified paper—one small step in DK's commitment to a sustainable future. For more information go to www.dk.com/our-green-pledge

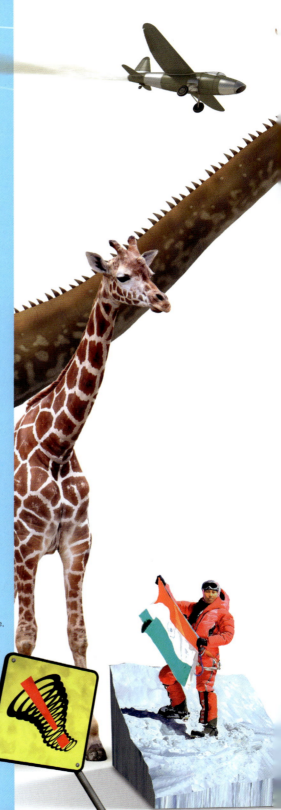

# 1,000 AMAZING RECORD BREAKERS

# CONTENTS

## 1 Planet Earth

Where on Earth? ............... 8
Where does everybody live? ................................. 10
Megacity .......................... 12
Violent volcanoes ............. 14
What a gem! .................... 16
Twister! ........................... 18
Deserts ............................ 20
An ocean of sand ............. 22
What a massive mine! ...... 24
Watery world ................... 26
Water data ....................... 28

## 2 People power

Who's in charge? .............. 32
Movie premieres .............. 34
Read all about it ............... 36
Adventurers ..................... 38
High achievers ................. 40
Arctic records .................. 42
Antarctic records ............. 44
I'm a survivor .................. 46

## 3 Sporting prowess

Olympic achievers ............
Goal!!! ..............................
Hot shots .........................
Home-run heroics ............
Kings of the road .............
Sports data ......................
Longest jump ..................
Raising the bar ................
100-meter marvels ..........
Lightning Bolt ..................
Amazing athletes .............
Perfect 10 ........................

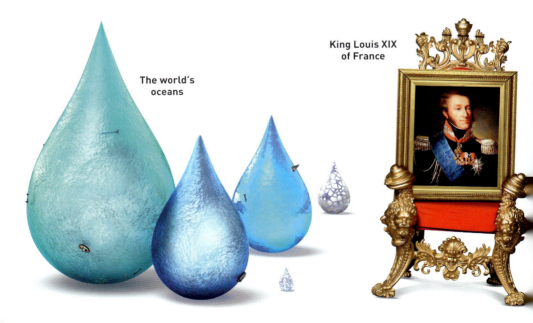

The world's oceans

King Louis XIX of France

## 4 Feats of engineering

| | |
|---|---|
| n the road | 76 |
| ll steam ahead | 78 |
| r pioneers | 80 |
| e need for speed | 82 |
| n the right track | 84 |
| vesome aircraft | 86 |
| ant of the sky | 88 |
| lossal collider | 90 |
| ega machines | 92 |
| onder walls | 94 |
| cord-breaking |  |
| ights | 96 |
| gineering data | 98 |

## 5 Living world

| | |
|---|---|
| Animal records | 102 |
| Life in the fast lane | 104 |
| Brilliant birds | 106 |
| Birds of a feather | 108 |
| A long way to go | 110 |
| Giants of the deep | 112 |
| Mini beasts | 114 |
| Super snakes | 116 |
| Rodent records | 118 |
| Prize-winning primates | 120 |
| Big babies | 122 |
| Longest life spans | 124 |
| Animal data | 126 |
| Awesome dinosaurs | 128 |
| The dinosaur tail continues | 130 |
| Prehistoric wonders | 132 |
| A *Tyrannosaurus* named Stan | 134 |
| Tree-mendous | 136 |
| Flower power | 138 |
| Leafy legends | 140 |
| Fantastic fruit | 142 |
| Flora and fungi data | 144 |

## 6 Out of this world

| | |
|---|---|
| Space records | 148 |
| Rocky planets | 150 |
| Snap-happy *Curiosity* | 152 |
| Jupiter the giant | 154 |
| The outer planets | 156 |
| Mooning around | 158 |
| Space rocks | 160 |
| First moon walk | 162 |
| Rocketing ahead | 164 |
| Sensational space station | 166 |
| The biggest dish | 168 |
| Space data | 170 |
| | |
| Index | 172 |
| Acknowledgments | 176 |

Europa

**Capybara**

Baluchistan pygmy jerboa

# Planet Earth

Nature is always the star of the show in planet Earth's most dazzling displays. From electric storms and erupting volcanoes to swirling tornadoes and spectacular seas, this record-breaking trip around the world shows nature in all its glory.

**Electrifying lightning strikes** light up the sky over Lake Maracaibo, Venezuela, on an average of 260 days of the year. There are about 640 lightning flashes per sq mile (250 per sq km) here—that's a higher density than anywhere else on Earth. On some nights, the lake sees 1,000 strikes an hour.

ANTARCTICA IS THE COLDEST, WINDIEST, AND DRIEST CONTINENT ON EARTH.

# WHERE ON EARTH?

Our planet is amazing! Most of the time it has just the **right conditions** for life. Some places, however, are very hot, really wet, or **incredibly snowy**.

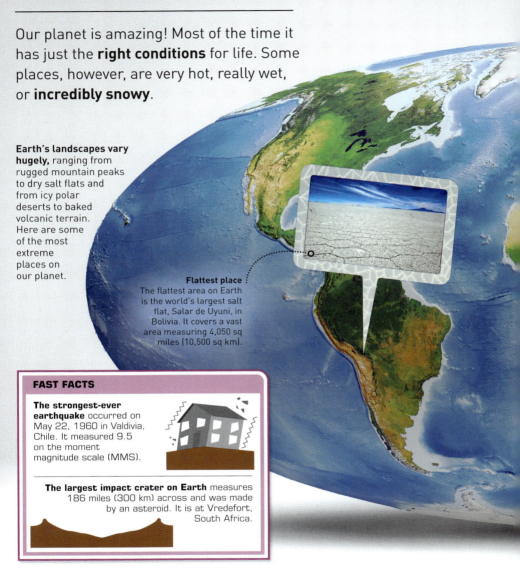

**Earth's landscapes vary hugely,** ranging from rugged mountain peaks to dry salt flats and from icy polar deserts to baked volcanic terrain. Here are some of the most extreme places on our planet.

**Flattest place**
The flattest area on Earth is the world's largest salt flat, Salar de Uyuni, in Bolivia. It covers a vast area measuring 4,050 sq miles (10,500 sq km).

### FAST FACTS

**The strongest-ever earthquake** occurred on May 22, 1960 in Valdivia, Chile. It measured 9.5 on the moment magnitude scale (MMS).

**The largest impact crater on Earth** measures 186 miles (300 km) across and was made by an asteroid. It is at Vredefort, South Africa.

**THE HOTTEST WATER TEMPERATURE OF 867°F (464°C) WAS RECORDED COMING FROM A HYDROTHERMAL VENT IN 2008.**

**LIGHTNING STRIKES EARTH 50–100 TIMES EVERY SECOND. EACH BOLT CAN HAVE A VOLTAGE OF UP TO 1 BILLION VOLTS.**

**AFRICA IS THE HOTTEST CONTINENT, WITH THE MOST HOURS OF SUNSHINE.**

**Hottest place**
The place with the world's highest average temperature is Dallol in Ethiopia, with a fiery 95°F (35°C). If that were not hot enough, there is a volcano here as well.

**Wettest place**
Mawsynram, in northern India, receives on average 467 in (1,187 cm) of rain each year. In 1860/1861, 1,042 in (2,647 cm) of rain fell on the nearby town of Cherrapunji, the largest ever recorded in a single year.

**Snowiest place**
In 1927, snow fell to a record depth of 465 in (1,182 cm) on Mount Ibuki, in Japan.

**The Mariana Trench** is the **deepest place** on the planet—**6.8 miles (11 km)** below sea level.

**Driest place**
The McMurdo Dry Valleys in Antarctica have had no water fall on them for 2 million years.

**Coldest place**
The Vostok Research Station in Antarctica recorded a temperature of –128.6°F (–89.2°C) on July 21, 1983.

AT –457°F (–272°C), THE BOOMERANG NEBULA BECAME THE COLDEST PLACE IN THE UNIVERSE WHEN MEASURED IN 1995.

QUASAR 3C273 IS THE HOTTEST PLACE IN THE UNIVERSE. TEMPERATURES THERE EXCEED 18 TRILLION °F.

**ANTARCTICA IS THE ONLY CONTINENT WITH NO NATIVE OR PERMANENT POPULATION.**

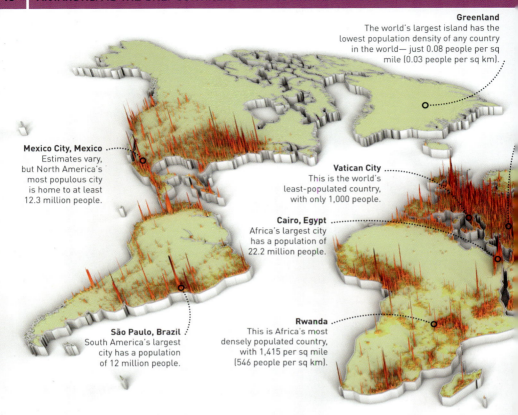

**Greenland**
The world's largest island has the lowest population density of any country in the world— just 0.08 people per sq mile (0.03 people per sq km).

**Mexico City, Mexico**
Estimates vary, but North America's most populous city is home to at least 12.3 million people.

**Vatican City**
This is the world's least-populated country, with only 1,000 people.

**Cairo, Egypt**
Africa's largest city has a population of 22.2 million people.

**São Paulo, Brazil**
South America's largest city has a population of 12 million people.

**Rwanda**
This is Africa's most densely populated country, with 1,415 per sq mile (546 people per sq km).

# WHERE DOES EVERYBODY LIVE?

The **world's population** is estimated to be **8.1 billion**. But which are the **most densely populated countries** on Earth, and where are each continent's **most-populous cities**?

**THE GLOBAL POPULATION REACHED 8 BILLION IN 2022. IN 1922, IT WAS AROUND 2 BILLION.**

**THE WORLD'S POPULATION IS PREDICTED TO GO PAST 10 BILLION PEOPLE BY THE 2060s.**

ABOUT 55 PERCENT OF THE GLOBAL POPULATION LIVE IN TOWNS AND CITIES.

**Istanbul, Türkiye**
With a population of 16.1 million people, this city is considered the largest in Europe, even though it has a foot in both Europe and Asia.

### PACKED TOGETHER

**Dhaka,** Bangladesh, is the most densely populated city on Earth. It has a massive population of around 18 million people, with 114,000 people per sq mile (44,000 people per sq km).

This map shows where people live on Earth. The height of each spike represents the number of people who live in a particular area. Southeast Asia, the Indian subcontinent, and northern Europe are the world's most densely populated areas.

**India**
This country has the world's joint-largest population (1.43 billion people). With a faster rate of population growth, it will soon overtake China as the most populous nation.

**China**
Like India, it has 1.43 billion inhabitants. That's around one-fifth of the world's population.

**Shanghai, China**
More people live inside this city's boundaries (29.2 million) than in any other city on Earth.

**Java**
Forming part of Indonesia, this is the world's most-populous island, with a population of 157.6 million people.

**Sydney, Australia**
The largest city in Australasia and Oceania, it has a population of 5.2 million people.

Almost **two-thirds** of the **world's population** live in **Asia**.

POPULATION GROWTH HAS BEEN DRIVEN BY PEOPLE **LIVING LONGER.** IN 1950, AVERAGE LIFE EXPECTANCY WAS 46.5; IT IS NOW 71.7 YEARS.

**AFRICA** HAS THE HIGHEST RATE OF POPULATION GROWTH. THE POPULATION OF SUB-SAHARAN AFRICA WILL DOUBLE BY 2050.

**MEGACITY**

**Located on the Yangtze River delta** along the middle of China's coastline, Shanghai is a major global financial center and home to the world's busiest container port. It also has more people living within its city boundaries than any other city in the world—at last count, an estimated 29.2 million people.

THE WORD "VOLCANO" COMES FROM VULCAN, THE ROMAN GOD OF FIRE.

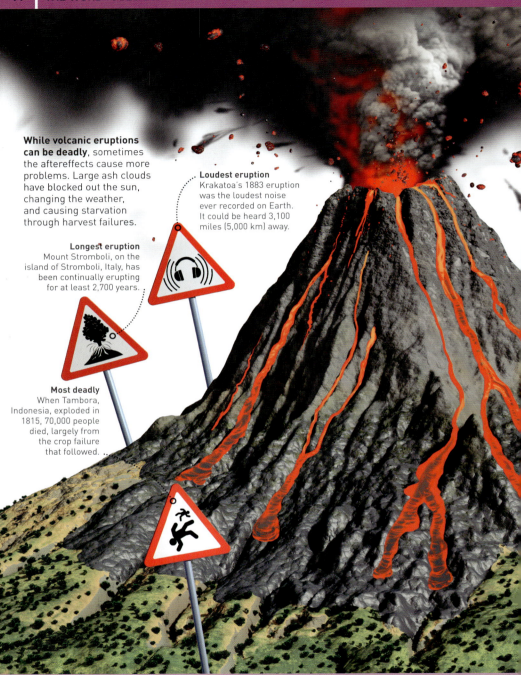

**While volcanic eruptions can be deadly**, sometimes the aftereffects cause more problems. Large ash clouds have blocked out the sun, changing the weather, and causing starvation through harvest failures.

**Loudest eruption**
Krakatoa's 1883 eruption was the loudest noise ever recorded on Earth. It could be heard 3,100 miles (5,000 km) away.

**Longest eruption**
Mount Stromboli, on the island of Stromboli, Italy, has been continually erupting for at least 2,700 years.

**Most deadly**
When Tambora, Indonesia, exploded in 1815, 70,000 people died, largely from the crop failure that followed.

 MORE THAN 80 PERCENT OF EARTH'S SURFACE HAS BEEN SHAPED BY BILLIONS OF YEARS OF VOLCANIC ACTIVITY.

 ABOUT 75 PERCENT OF THE WORLD'S VOLCANOES ERUPT IN THE RING OF FIRE IN THE PACIFIC OCEAN.

IN 2017, SCIENTISTS FOUND 91 VOLCANOES UNDER THE ICE OF ANTARCTICA.

# VIOLENT VOLCANOES

Rock-shattering **explosions**, burning **lava**, choking **ash clouds**—all volcanoes are **dangerous**, but which are the most **extreme** of all?

Of the world's **1,500** potentially active volcanoes, **20** are **erupting** at any one time.

**Largest eruption**
Mount Toba erupted about 75,000 years ago in an explosion 100 times bigger than Krakatoa in 1883. It spewed out about 672 cubic miles (2,800 cubic km) of debris.

**Fastest lava flow**
Mount Nyiragongo, in the Democratic Republic of Congo, has the largest lava lake, which in 1977 caused the fastest lava flow: 37 mph (60 km/h).

### FAST FACTS

**The countries with the most volcanoes** are the US (173) and Russia (166). They are both big countries, but the main reason they have so many volcanoes is that they touch the "Ring of Fire." This is an imaginary line around the Pacific Ocean where most volcanoes occur. The line also goes through Indonesia, Japan, and Chile.

US 173
Russia 166
Indonesia 139
Japan 112
Chile 104

**FAST-FLOWING ROCK AND ASH FROM ERUPTING VOLCANOES CAN REACH SPEEDS OF 435 MPH (700 KM/H).**

**WHEN TAMBORA ERUPTED, ASH CLOUDS AND SULFATES BLOCKED THE SUN AND CAUSED THE "YEAR WITHOUT SUMMER."**

**THERE ARE AROUND 200 DIFFERENT KINDS OF GEMSTONES.**

# WHAT A GEM!

Here is a collection of some of the world's most precious **gemstones**. Some are **very valuable** because they are so huge; others are **rare** and have been **elegantly cut** to bring out their beauty.

**Largest pearl ever found**
A fisherman in the Philippines discovered this giant pearl weighing 75 lb (34 kg) in 2006. It is thought to have come from a giant clam.

**World's most expensive gemstone**
A beautiful pink star diamond was sold at auction in 2017 for a staggering $71.2 million (£57.3 million). This very high quality stone weighs 59.6 carats.

**World's largest blue star sapphire**
This egg-shaped gem was found in Sri Lanka in 2015. When a light is shone on it, a six-sided star appears. It weighs 1,404.49 carats and is named the Star of Adam.

MEXICO'S **CAVE OF THE CRYSTALS** HOUSES RECORD-BREAKING CRYSTALS THAT MEASURE OVER 33 FT (10 M) LONG.

NAMED AFTER THE GREEK WORD FOR "UNBREAKABLE," **DIAMONDS** ARE THE HARDEST NATURALLY OCCURRING SUBSTAN

**AT 4.4 BILLION YEARS OLD, ZIRCON IS EARTH'S MOST ANCIENT GEMSTONE.**

**Biggest opal in the world**
This giant piece of opal came from a mine in south Australia in 1956. It was named Olympic Australis and weighs 17,000 carats.

**Biggest gold nugget**
Called the Welcome Stranger, this nugget was discovered by two miners in Victoria, Australia, in 1869. It weighed 145 lb (66 kg).

**Largest cut diamond in the world**
A huge yellow stone called the Golden Jubilee was found in a diamond mine in South Africa in 1985. It was cut into a sparkling gem weighing 545.67 carats.

### FAST FACTS

**Gemstones are usually weighed** in carats. One carat is roughly equivalent to the weight of a drop of water. Some gigantic gems weigh the same as some birds or small animals.

|  | |  |
|---|---|---|
| **1 carat** 0.007 oz (0.2 g) | 💧 | A drop of water |
| **50 carats** 0.3 oz (10 g) | | Two hummingbirds |
| **100 carats** 0.7 oz (20 g) | | Barn swallow |
| **1,000 carats** 7 oz (200 g) | | American red squirrel |
| **5,000 carats** 35 oz (1,000 g) | | Black-footed ferret |
| **10,000 carats** 70 oz (2,000 g) | | Ring-tailed lemur |

**DURING THE 1840S GOLD RUSH IN THE US, THE YELLOW MINERAL PYRITE BECAME KNOWN AS "FOOL'S GOLD."**

**THE WORLD'S LARGEST UNCUT EMERALD WAS FOUND IN ZAMBIA IN 2021. IT WEIGHS 3.3 LB (1.5 KG).**

# TWISTER!

**Spinning** along the ground at up to **70 mph** (110 km/h) and reaching up to the **clouds**, a strong **tornado sucks up** whatever lies in its path, causing **devastation**.

**Fastest wind**
During a 1999 tornado in Oklahoma, wind speeds inside the funnel reached 301 mph (484 km/h) at 330 ft (100 m) above the ground.

**A tornado forms** when warm, moist air near the ground meets cool, dry air above, making the warm air rise up in a spinning column. Large tornadoes can rotate as quickly as 300 mph (480 km/h), be 2.5 miles (4 km) wide, and last for 30 minutes while tearing across the landscape and destroying anything in their path.

### TORNADO CHASING

The dangerous pastime of storm-chasing involves following storms and tornadoes to photograph them and record data. American David Hoadley is credited as the pioneer of storm-chasing. He started in 1956 and has seen more than 230 tornadoes.

**Deadliest tornado**
In Bangladesh in April 1989, the Daulatpur-Saturia tornado destroyed trees and houses over 2.3 sq miles (6 sq km), killing 1,300 people and injuring thousands more.

**ABOUT 30 PERCENT OF TORNADOES** IN THE US HIT "TORNADO ALLEY," A REGION SPANNING FOUR CENTRAL AND SOUTHERN STATES.

300,000 MPH (500,000 KM/H): TOP SPEED OF TORNADOES IN THE SUN'S ATMOSPHERE.

... AND COUNTERCLOCKWISE IN THE NORTHERN HEMISPHERE.

The world's longest-lasting tornado blew for 3.5 hours across three US states in 1925.

**Longest distance carried by a tornado**
A tornado that struck Missouri, on March 12, 2006, swept up a trailer with Matt Suter inside. It was carried 1,307 ft (398 m). Matt Suter fell out at some point but lived to tell the tale!

**Most tornadoes**
In 2011, a "super outbreak" of tornadoes hit 21 US states and parts of southern Canada. In total, there were 362 tornadoes over 72 hours, causing damage worth $11 billion (£7.9 billion).

**Widest tornado path**
In 2013, the El Reno tornado carved a path through Oklahoma, 2.6 miles (4.2 km) wide—officially the widest on record.

 **WATERSPOUTS ARE TORNADOES THAT FORM OVER WATER AND CAUSE CHAOS IF THEY REACH THE SHORE.**

 **TORNADOES ARE RATED ON THE ENHANCED FUJITA SCALE FROM F0 UP TO F5 FOR THE MOST DANGEROUS.**

**MORE THAN 1 BILLION PEOPLE LIVE IN DESERTS AROUND THE WORLD.**

### Hottest desert
### Death Valley, Mojave

**The highest land temperature** ever recorded was at Furnace Creek in Death Valley, California. On July 10, 1913, the temperature reached 134°F (56.7°C).

### Driest desert
### Atacama

**Some weather stations** across the Atacama Desert, in Chile, have never recorded a drop of rain. The average rainfall across the desert is 0.6 in (15 mm) per year.

### Largest sand desert
### Rub' al Khali

**Also known as the Empty Quarter,** the Rub' al Khali, which forms part of the Arabian Desert, is the largest continuous sand desert in the world.

**ANTARCTICA** IS A DESERT THAT CONTAINS AROUND 80 PERCENT OF THE WORLD'S FRESH WATER SUPPLY.

PARTS OF THE **ATACAMA DESERT** MAY HAVE GONE WITHOUT RAIN FOR 40 MILLION YEARS.

MARS IS THE ONLY PLANET WITH DESERT LANDSCAPES SIMILAR TO EARTH'S. 21

**Biggest desert**
Antarctica

**The Antarctic Desert** is the world's largest. It covers 5.5 million sq miles (14.2 million sq km), more than one-and-a-half times the size of the Sahara Desert.

**Oldest desert**
Namib

Having endured arid conditions for 55 to 80 million years, southern Africa's Namib Desert is thought to be the oldest in the world.

# DESERTS

A **desert** is a place that receives **less than 10 in (25 cm) of rain** per year. But not all deserts are hot. The **world's largest desert** is found in freezing **Antarctica**.

**Deserts can be found** on every one of the world's continents and cover more than one-fifth of land on Earth. Surprisingly, only 10 percent of the world's deserts are covered by sand.

TEMPERATURES IN NORTHERN AFRICA'S SAHARA DESERT GO FROM 100°F (38°C) BY DAY TO 25°F (−4°C) AT NIGHT.

THE **NAMIBIAN DESERT BEETLE** SURVIVES BY EXTRACTING AND DRINKING WATER FROM LOW-LYING FOG.

## AN OCEAN OF SAND

**The Rub' al Khali, also known as the "Empty Quarter,"** is the largest area of continuous sand in the world. Forming part of the Arabian Desert, it covers 251,000 sq miles (650,000 sq km)—an area larger than France.

ABOUT 16 PERCENT OF US COPPER PRODUCTION COMES FROM BINGHAM CANYON.

**Copper mine**
The mine is thought to have produced more copper than any other mine in history: as much as 19 million tons (17.2 million metric tons).

**Empire State Building**
The towering Empire State Building in New York is 1,250 ft (381 m) tall. This means it would take more than three of them to reach the top of the Bingham Canyon mine.

**This vast open-pit mine** is the largest man-made excavation on Earth. The mining of copper began here in 1906 and now the mine covers 1,900 acres (770 hectares)—which is equivalent to the size of a small town.

# WHAT A
# MASSIVE MINE!

**Bingham Canyon mine**, Utah, is a **massive crater** 3,937 ft (1,200 m) deep and more than **2.5 miles (4 km) wide**. The mine produces **copper**, gold, silver, and a metal called molybdenum.

 UNTIL THE LANDSLIDE MADE THE MINE UNSAFE, **3 MILLION TOURISTS** VISITED BINGHAM CANYON BETWEEN 1992 AND 2012.

TECHNOLOGY DETECTED THE LANDSLIDE IN ADVANCE, SO NO ONE WAS HURT.

THE WORLD'S OLDEST MINE, IN EGYPT, WAS FIRST USED 100,000 YEARS AGO.

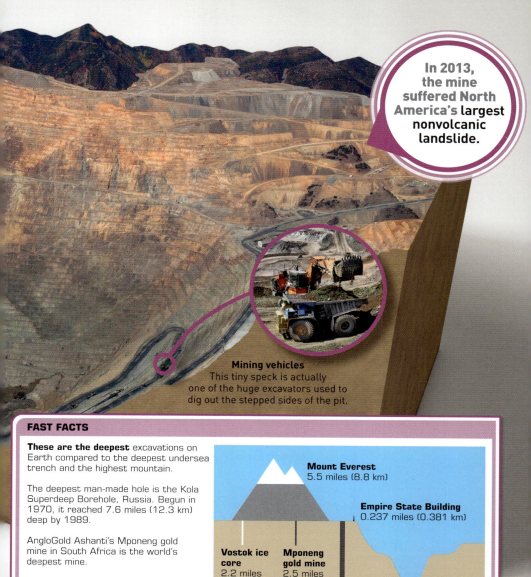

In 2013, the mine suffered North America's largest nonvolcanic landslide.

**Mining vehicles**
This tiny speck is actually one of the huge excavators used to dig out the stepped sides of the pit.

## FAST FACTS

**These are the deepest** excavations on Earth compared to the deepest undersea trench and the highest mountain.

The deepest man-made hole is the Kola Superdeep Borehole, Russia. Begun in 1970, it reached 7.6 miles (12.3 km) deep by 1989.

AngloGold Ashanti's Mponeng gold mine in South Africa is the world's deepest mine.

The deepest ice core (2.2 miles/3.6 km) was drilled at the Vostok Research station, East Antarctica.

**Mount Everest** 5.5 miles (8.8 km)

**Empire State Building** 0.237 miles (0.381 km)

**Vostok ice core** 2.2 miles (3.6 km)

**Mponeng gold mine** 2.5 miles (4 km)

**Kola Superdeep Borehole** 7.6 miles (12.3 km)

**Mariana Trench** 6.8 miles (11 km)

IN 2011, THE TOTAL VALUE OF ALL THE METALS MINED AT BINGHAM CANYON WAS A STAGGERING **$2.9** BILLION.

THE DEEPEST ELEVATOR IN A MINE SHAFT DESCENDS 1.4 MILES (2.28 KM) AT SOUTH AFRICA'S MPONENG GOLD MINE

**THE PACIFIC OCEAN COVERS ONE-THIRD OF EARTH'S SURFACE.**

# WATERY WORLD

Earth is a **blue planet**, with more than **two-thirds** of the surface covered in **water**. These **oceans** contain **97 percent** of all our **water**. Dive in to discover the oceans **making waves** around the world.

**The five named oceans** are the Pacific, Atlantic, Indian, Southern, and Arctic. They are all connected around the seven continents, so in reality there is only one vast ocean covering our world.

### SHRINKING SEA

The Aral Sea (actually a freshwater lake in central Asia) was once the fourth-largest lake in the world, but it is shrinking fast. In 2014, its eastern basin (seen to the right of the image) dried up for what is thought to be the first time in 600 years.

*Pacific Ocean*

**160,700,000 cubic miles**
(669,880,000 cubic km)

**The record-breaking Pacific** is easily the biggest ocean, holding more than half of the world's seawater. All of Earth's continents could fit comfortably inside the Pacific Basin. It is also the deepest ocean. What's more, about 75 percent of the world's volcanoes are found beneath its waters.

**THE OCEANS FIRST FORMED ABOUT 3.8 BILLION YEARS AGO WHEN RAIN FELL INTO HOLLOWS ON EARTH'S SURFACE.**

**A STONE DROPPED INTO THE DEPTHS OF THE PACIFIC OCEAN WOULD TAKE MORE THAN AN HOUR TO REACH THE BOTTOM.**

THE OCEANS ARE HOME TO MORE THAN 225,000 SPECIES OF MARINE LIFE.

### FAST FACTS

**The deepest parts** of the oceans are shown in this chart. The Mariana Trench, in the Pacific, is the deepest point on Earth; if Mount Everest was dropped inside, its summit would still be more than 1 mile (2 km) below the ocean surface.

Depth in feet:
- −6,600
- −13,000
- −20,000
- −26,000
- −33,000
- −39,000

- Mariana Trench, Pacific: 36,198 ft (11,033 m)
- Puerto Rico Trench, Atlantic: 28,374 ft (8,648 m)
- Java Trench, Indian: 25,344 ft (7,725 m)
- South Sandwich Trench, Southern: 24,390 ft (7,434 m)
- Litke Deep, Arctic: 17,881 ft (5,450 m)

**The Pacific Ocean contains more water than all the other oceans combined.**

**Atlantic Ocean**

**Indian Ocean**

**Southern Ocean**

**17,225,730 cubic miles** (71,800,000 cubic km)

**63,340,000 cubic miles** (264,000,000 cubic km)

**More people live on the shores** of the Indian Ocean than any other. About one-third of the global population have set up home here, enjoying the world's warmest waters, where the temperature can reach 82°F (28°C).

**74,471,500 cubic miles** (310,410,900 cubic km)

**Coming second to the Pacific**, the Atlantic is the next largest ocean and also the saltiest sea. These bountiful waters are known for gas, oil, and fish. The Atlantic widens by up to 4 in (10 cm) every year as the continental plates beneath its surface move farther apart.

**Surrounding icy Antarctica**, the Southern Ocean was considered an extension of the bigger oceans until it was officially given its name in 2000.

**4,500,000 cubic miles** (18,750,000 cubic km)

**Arctic Ocean**

**Just a drop in the ocean** compared to the others, the Arctic Ocean is the smallest, the shallowest, and has the least salty waters.

**PORTUGUESE NAVIGATOR FERDINAND MAGELLAN NAMED THE PACIFIC ("PEACEFUL") OCEAN IN 1520.**

**ONLY ABOUT 5 PERCENT OF THE OCEANS HAVE BEEN EXPLORED AND VISITED BY HUMANS.**

THERE ARE MORE THAN 165 RIVERS LONGER THAN 621 MILES (1,000 KM).

# Water data

The **salinity**, or **saltiness**, of water is measured in **"parts per thousand" (ppt)**—that is, how many grams of salt there are in **1,000 g of water**. It is also expressed as a percentage, so **Gaet'ale Pond** has a salinity of **43.3 percent**.

**433 PPT GAET'ALE POND** ETHIOPIA THE SALTIEST WATER ON EARTH

**337 PPT DEAD SEA** ISRAEL/JORDAN

**403 PPT DON JUAN LAKE** ANTARCTICA

**270 PPT GREAT SALT LAKE** USA

## SALTIEST WATER

**BRINY WATER** 50+ PPT

**SALINE WATER** 30 PPT

**BRACKISH WATER** 0.5 PPT

**FRESH WATER** 0 PPT

- 38 PPT MEDITERRANEAN SEA
- 35 PPT PACIFIC AND ATLANTIC OCEANS
- 2 PPT LIMIT ALLOWED FOR WATERING CROPS
- 0.1 PPT DRINKING WATER

## TALLEST WATERFALLS

The **world's tallest waterfall is under water!** Lying in the **DENMARK STRAIT** between **GREENLAND** and **ICELAND**, the **DENMARK STRAIT CATARACT** is more than **three and a half times taller** than **ANGEL FALLS**, the tallest waterfall on land.

OVERFLOW
SEA FLOOR

DENMARK CATARACT, DENMARK STRAIT 11,500 FT (3,505 M)
ANGEL FALLS, VENEZUELA 3,212 FT (979 M)
EIFFEL TOWER 1,063 FT (321 M)

## DEEPEST LAKE

Although **Lake Baikal** is the **seventh-largest** lake by area, it is so deep it **holds one-fifth** of all the unfrozen fresh water in the world: **5,700 cu miles (23,600 cu km)**. Baikal is on average **2,487 ft (758 m)** deep. But at its **deepest**, it sinks to **5,387 ft (1,642 m)**—that's as deep as two Burj Khalifas.

BAIKAL—AVERAGE DEPTH 2,487 FT (758 M).
BURJ KHALIFA—2,717 FT (828 M)

**MEASURING 4,100 MILES (6,600 KM), THE NILE IN AFRICA IS THE WORLD'S LONGEST RIVER.**

IN 2020, GERMAN SEBASTIAN STEUDTN SURFED THE BIGGES **WAVE**. IT MEASURED 86 FT (26 M) AND WAS IN NAZARÉ, PORTUGA

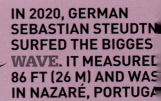

AT 33,497 FT (10,210 M), MAUNA KEA IS THE TALLEST MOUNTAIN IN THE OCEAN.

## RAINY RÉUNION

Several **tropical cyclones** have set different records for rainfall on **Réunion Island** in the Indian Ocean.

- 12 HRS — DENISE, JANUARY 1966 — 71.9 IN (182.5 CM)
- 24 HRS — (UNNAMED CYCLONE), APRIL 1958–97 IN (246.7 CM)
- 48 HRS — GAMEDE, FEBRUARY 2007 — 154.6 IN (393 CM)
- 72 HRS — HYACINTHE, JANUARY 1980 — 239.5 IN (608 CM)
- 15 DAYS

3.5 TIMES THE HEIGHT OF AN AVERAGE PERSON

**SATELLITE IMAGERY** in use since 1970 has revealed the **most hurricane-hit countries in THE WORLD**: China, the Philippines, Japan, Mexico, and the US.

## WILD WATERSPOUTS

A COLUMN OF CLOUD-FILLED WIND WHIRLING OVER WATER IS CALLED A WATERSPOUT.

TORNADIC WATERSPOUTS DEVELOP AND SWIRL DOWN FROM THE CLOUDS, RATHER THAN UP FROM THE WATER.

MOST ARE SMALL, AROUND 165 FT (50 M) IN DIAMETER, AND LAST FOR JUST A FEW MINUTES.

THE BIGGEST CAN BE UP TO 330 FT (100 M) IN DIAMETER AND LAST UP TO AN HOUR.

## WATER SPEED

Running alongside the coast of the **US, the Gulf Stream**—a current in the **North Atlantic Ocean**—flows at **4 mph (6.4 km/h)**. Sounds slow? It's still **four times faster** than the **Amazon River's** flow rate.

## LARGEST LAKE PER CONTINENT

These are the **biggest lakes** on each continent, by **surface area**.

- **CASPIAN SEA** (ASIA) 143,000 SQ MILES (371,000 SQ KM)
- **LAKE SUPERIOR** (NORTH AMERICA) 31,700 SQ MILES (82,100 SQ KM)
- **LAKE VICTORIA** (AFRICA) 26,590 SQ MILES (68,870 SQ KM)
- **LAKE LADOGA** (EUROPE) 7,000 SQ MILES (18,130 SQ KM)
- **LAKE VOSTOK** (ANTARTICA) 4,800 SQ MILES (12,500 SQ KM)
- **LAKE EYRE** (OCEANIA) 3,670 SQ MILES (9,500 SQ KM)
- **LAKE TITICACA** (SOUTH AMERICA) 3,232 SQ MILES (8,372 SQ KM)

**720** — THE CONGO RIVER DROPS TO **720 FT (220 M)** AT ITS DEEPEST, AND IT CROSSES 10 AFRICAN COUNTRIES.

THE WORLD'S ONLY UNDERWATER POST OFFICE, **VANUATU POST** SITS OFF THE PACIFIC ISLAND NATION OF VANUATU.

# People power

Today planet Earth is home to more than 8 billion people. Those that stand out from the crowd challenge themselves by relentlessly pursuing their dreams. Trailblazers strive to make history, adventurers explore uncharted territory, and leaders rule entire nations.

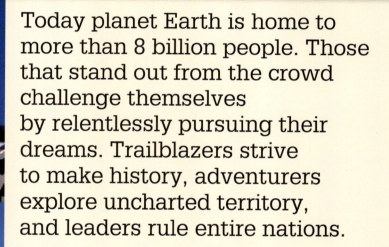

**American Jordan Romero** was 13 years 10 months and 10 days old when he reached the summit of Mount Everest on May 22, 2010. In doing so, he became the youngest person in history to climb the world's highest mountain. In December 2011, he went on to become the youngest to climb each of the Seven Summits— the highest peaks in each continental plate.

THE FIRST ROYAL PALACE WAS BUILT IN EGYPT AROUND 3000 BCE.

**Longest-ruling royal house**
Naruhito is the current emperor of Japan. He is 126th in line from the first emperor, Jimmu, whose ascension is officially dated at 660 BCE. This means the same royal house has ruled Japan for more than 2,600 years!

**Shortest-reigning monarch**
Blink and you could miss the reign of Louis-Antoine of France! In 1830, he took the French throne as King Louis XIX, but abdicated 20 minutes later.

**Longest verifiable reign**
Sobhuza II reigned as king of Swaziland for 82 years and 254 days. After his father died, he became monarch at four months old in 1899 and remained king until his own death in 1982.

**From kings and queens** to prime ministers and presidents, the most memorable leaders are usually those who served their countries the longest or took charge during challenging periods of conflict and change.

### FAST FACTS

**The longest-serving US president** was Franklin D. Roosevelt, who took charge for 4,422 days from 1933 to 1945, and remains the only US president to serve three full terms.

**The shortest-serving US president** was William Henry Harrison who died of pneumonia in 1841, just 31 days after his inauguration.

**Longest-reigning monarch today**
Sultan Hassanal Bolkiah of Brunei is now the world's longest-serving monarch, following the death of Queen Elizabeth II in 2022.

A RECORD-BREAKING **144** RULERS, PRIME MINISTERS, AND PRESIDENTS MET AT A UNITED NATIONS SUMMIT IN 2000.

THE LONGEST ROYAL WEDDING PROCESSION TOOK PLACE IN JORDAN IN 2023, AND MEASURED 6 MILES (9.7 KM).

ELIZABETH II WAS THE OLDEST REIGNING QUEEN. SHE DIED AT AGE 96 IN 2022.

**First female head of state**
Sirimavo Bandaranaike became the world's first female head of state when her party, the Sri Lanka Freedom Party, won the Sri Lankan elections in July 1960.

**Longest-reigning non-royal leader since 1900**
Ancient leaders may have served for longer, but the modern-day winner is Fidel Castro. The Cuban prime minister and president served for 52 years and 62 days, from 1959 until 2011.

**Longest-serving female head of state**
Vigdís Finnbogadóttir was president of Iceland for a record-breaking 16 years from August 1, 1980, to 1996—a record for a female head of state.

**More than 100 women have become prime ministers and presidents since 1960.**

# WHO'S IN CHARGE?

From the **longest-reigning monarch** to the **first female head of state**, please be upstanding for the **royal rulers** and **powerhouse politicians** who have led their nations into the history books.

**THE YOUNGEST REIGNING MONARCH IS KING OYO, WHO HAS RULED TORO, A KINGDOM IN UGANDA, SINCE HE WAS THREE.**

**FORTY-THREE COUNTRIES IN THE WORLD STILL HAVE A KING OR QUEEN AS THEIR OFFICIAL HEAD OF STATE.**

# MOVIE PREMIERES

From the moment the Lumière brothers **first** presented a projected **motion picture** to a paying public in Paris on December 28, 1895, **movies** have become a major form of **social entertainment**.

**Avengers: Endgame** earned $157,461,641 (£122,945,262) on its opening day at the cinema in 2019, the highest amount ever made by any movie.

### MILLION-DOLLAR LADY

In 1916, Mary Pickford became the first actor or actress in history to receive a million-dollar contract in Hollywood. The Canadian-born actress starred in 52 feature films.

**Jaws**, director Steven Spielberg's 1975 movie about a man-eating shark, was the first film in history to make more than $100 million (£79.64 million) at the box office.

MADE IN 1888 BY FRENCH INVENTOR LOUIS LE PRINCE, *ROUNDHAY GARDEN SCENE* IS THE WORLD'S OLDEST FILM. IT IS TWO SECONDS LONG.

**47** RAMOJI FILM CITY NEAR HYDERABAD, INDIA, IS THE WORLD'S BIGGEST MOVIE STUDIO, WITH **47** SOUND STAGES.

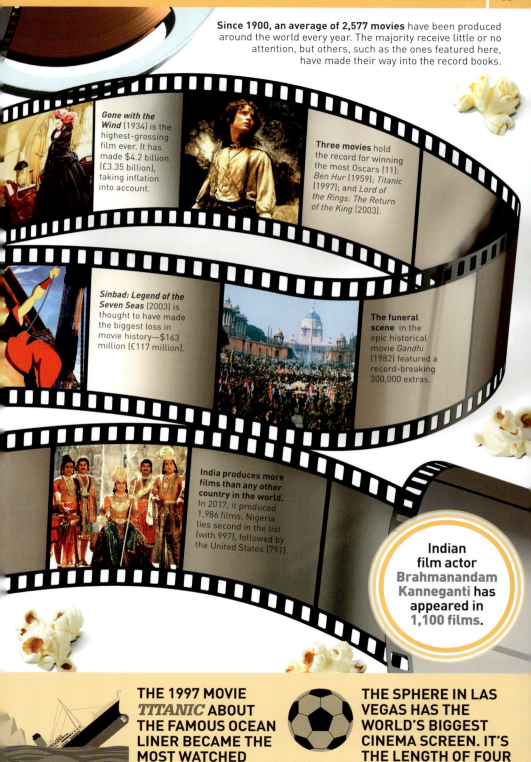

THE FIRST CROSSWORD PUZZLE BOOK WAS PUBLISHED IN 1924 IN THE US.

# READ ALL ABOUT IT

Around 2.21 million books are published throughout the world each year, but which book has sold more than any other, who are the bestselling authors of all time, and which have been the world's most successful comics?

**Best selling series**

*The Harry Potter* series of books

J. K. Rowling's series of books about a young wizard has sold more than 600 million copies.

**Bestselling regularly updated book**

Xinhua Dictionary

First published in 1953, this Chinese dictionary has sold around 400 million copies.

**Bestselling cookbook**

*Betty Crocker's Cookbook*

First published in 1950, more than 75 million copies of this American cookbook have been sold.

**Bestselling writers**

William Shakespeare
Agatha Christie

Two English authors, playwright William Shakespeare (1564–1616) and crime writer Agatha Christie (1890–1976; right), are both thought to have sold at least two billion books. Shakespeare wrote 37 plays, and Christie penned 78 crime books and other books and short stories.

THE MOST OVERDUE LIBRARY **BOOK** WAS BORROWED IN 1668 AND RETURNED IN 1956!

 *THE LITTLE PRINCE* IS THE BESTSELLING CHILDREN'S BOOK OF ALL TIME. AT LEAST 200 MILLION COPIES OF IT HAVE BEEN BOUGHT.

THE LONGEST BOOK TITLE IS A WHOPPING 27,978 LETTERS LONG!

Everyone loves a **good book**, so find a seat and browse through these **record-breaking classics**.

### Bestselling nonfiction book
**The Bible**
Figures are impossible to verify, but it is thought that around 5 billion copies of the Bible have been sold.

### Most translated author
**Agatha Christie**
According to UNESCO, there have been an astonishing 7,236 translations of Agatha Christie books—more than for any author in history.

### Most expensive book ever sold
**"Codex Sassoon"**
Sold at auction for $38.1 million (£30.3 million) in 2023, this almost complete Hebrew Bible is thought to date back to the 9th century.

### Bestselling comics
**Micky Maus (Germany), The Beano, and Classics Illustrated (both English language)**
Each of these comics (picture books) are thought to have sold 1 billion copies.

### Bestselling fiction book
**Don Quixote**
First published in 1605 in Spain, Miguel de Cervantes' story of the nobleman Don Quixote and his companion Sancho Panza has sold an estimated 500 million copies.

More **books** are published in **China** per year than in any other country—440,000 in 2013.

**SEVEN-VOLUME *IN SEARCH OF LOST TIME* IS THE LONGEST-EVER BOOK. IT HAS 1.3 MILLION WORDS.**

**THE *DIARY OF ANNE FRANK* HAS SOLD MORE THAN 30 MILLION COPIES IN 70 LANGUAGES.**

**First woman to fly solo from Britain to Australia** In May 1930, Englishwoman Amy Johnson took off in her Gipsy Moth plane from an airstrip in Croydon, England. She flew 11,000 miles (17,700 km) to land in Darwin, Australia, 19 days later. The first person to fly solo from Britain to Australia was Australian Bert Hinkler in 1928.

> Earhart was the **first woman** to fly across the Atlantic Ocean in 1928—as a passenger.

**First woman to fly solo across the Atlantic Ocean** Another flier, America's Amelia Earhart, flew across the Atlantic Ocean in May 1932. The trip from Canada to Northern Ireland took 15 hours. Charles Lindbergh was the first person to complete the flight solo in his plane *Spirit of St. Louis* in 1927.

**First deep dive** Americans William Beebe and Otis Barton ventured deep underwater inside a submersible called a bathysphere in 1934. They descended to a depth of 3,028 ft (922 m).

# ADVENTURERS

These brave individuals **pushed the limits** of experience by **venturing farther** than anyone had gone before. Some **set off alone**; others traveled **higher or deeper** into the unknown.

IN 2002, AMERICAN STEVE FOSSETT MADE HISTORY WITH THE FIRST SOLO AROUND-THE-WORLD FLIGHT IN A **HOT AIR BALLOON**.

THE FIRST HOT-AIR BALLOON FLIGHT IN 1783 HAD ONLY A **SHEEP, DUCK, AND ROOSTER** ON BOARD!

12 MEN HAVE WALKED ON THE MOON, INCLUDING THE TWO APOLLO 11 ASTRONAUTS.

TANZANIA
BATHYSCAPHE TRIESTE 1960

### First to reach the deepest part of the ocean
Jacques Piccard from Switzerland and American Don Walsh were the first to reach the bottom of the Mariana Trench, a place called Challenger Deep, which is the very deepest part of the ocean. In 1960, they traveled in a bathyscaphe named *Trieste*, to a depth of 35,814 ft (10,916 m).

### First person to sail the world making just one stop
Englishman Francis Chichester left Plymouth, England, in August 1966. After 107 days, he reached Sydney, Australia, then returned via Cape Horn, taking 119 days and covering 29,630 miles (47,685 km) in total.

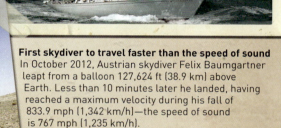

### First skydiver to travel faster than the speed of sound
In October 2012, Austrian skydiver Felix Baumgartner leapt from a balloon 127,624 ft (38.9 km) above Earth. Less than 10 minutes later he landed, having reached a maximum velocity during his fall of 833.9 mph (1,342 km/h)—the speed of sound is 767 mph (1,235 km/h).

**These adventurers** planned their journeys for months or years before they set off. Often the vehicles or vessels they traveled in had to be tested and adapted for the trip first.

### FAST FACTS

**The record set** by Felix Baumgartner was beaten in 2014 by former Google executive Alan Eustace, who leapt from 135,827 ft (41.4 km)—8,202 ft (2.5 km) higher than Baumgartner. Both jumped from the stratosphere, which starts at 9 miles (14.5 km) above Earth. Jumbo jets fly at 39,000 ft (11.8 km).

**Alan Eustace**
135,827 ft (41.4 km)

**Felix Baumgartner**
127,624 ft (38.9 km)

**Jumbo Jet**
39,000 ft (11.8 km)

IN 2023, CROATIAN PETAR KLOVAR MADE THE DEEPEST-EVER FREEDIVE OF **420 FT** (128 M) AT CEBU IN THE PHILIPPINES.

SWISS BRAZILIAN LAZARO SCHALLER ACHIEVED THE HIGHEST **DIVE** FROM A DIVING BOARD, PLUNGING 193 FT (59 M) IN 2015.

MORE THAN 6,000 PEOPLE HAVE REACHED THE SUMMIT OF EVEREST.

# HIGH ACHIEVERS

Scaling **Everest**, the **highest mountain** on Earth, must surely be the **peak** of these adventurers' achievements.

**1975**
The first female to the top was Junko Tabei (Japan), while Lhakpa Sherpa (Nepal) has summited 10 times.

**1953**
Sir Edmund Hillary (New Zealand) and Tenzing Norgay (Nepal) are officially the first people ever to reach the summit.

**2001**
The first person to descend on a snowboard was Marco Siffredi (France). He achieved the feat in 2001 but died while trying to repeat the descent the following year.

**2001**
The first blind explorer to the peak was Erik Weihenmayer (US), who has also conquered all of the Seven Summits.

**Although the first successful** ascent of Mount Everest occurred more than 70 years ago, there are many more records to be had, from the first woman to the youngest person; and then there are the descents, too.

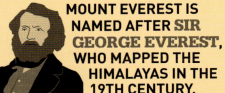

MOUNT EVEREST IS NAMED AFTER **SIR GEORGE EVEREST**, WHO MAPPED THE HIMALAYAS IN THE 19TH CENTURY.

PLATE TECTONICS BEGAN TO FORM THE **HIMALAYAS** MORE THAN 60 MILLION YEARS AGO.

MORE THAN 300 PEOPLE HAVE DIED CLIMBING THIS GIANT MOUNTAIN.

**1933**
**First to fly** over the peak were pilots Lord Clydesdale (Douglas Douglas-Hamilton) and David McIntyre, in a two-seater biplane.

### SPEEDY SUMMIT

In 2017, Spanish climber Kilian Jornet ascended Everest twice in one week without ropes or oxygen. He set the fastest time from Advance Base Camp (at 21,000 ft/6,400 m) to the summit: 17 hours. It normally takes four days.

**1993**
Aged 19, India's **Dicky Dolma** was the first female teenager to climb Everest. The youngest climber to date is 13-year-old American Jordan Romero.

**2013**
Aged 80, Yuichiro Miura of Japan is the oldest man to summit. He is 7 years older than Tamae Watanabe, the oldest woman to the top.

**1922**
**First attempts**, led by Charles G. Bruce and Edward Lisle Strutt (both from England), didn't reach the summit but set a world record for the highest climb: 27,320 ft (8,326 m).

Yuichiro Miura, **the oldest person to summit,** broke the record at age **70,** at **75,** and again at **80!**

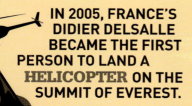

IN 2005, FRANCE'S DIDIER DELSALLE BECAME THE FIRST PERSON TO LAND A **HELICOPTER** ON THE SUMMIT OF EVEREST.

ALSO IN 2005, TWO BRAVE NEPALESE MOUNTAINEERS MADE HISTORY WHEN THEY **MARRIED** AT THE TOP OF MOUNT EVEREST!

THE ARCTIC IS HOME TO ABOUT 4 MILLION PEOPLE, INCLUDING THE NATIVE INUIT.

**First to sail the Northwest Passage**
In 1906, Norwegian explorer Roald Amundsen (far left) became the first to sail through this important trade route across the Arctic, which connects the Atlantic and Pacific Oceans.

**First to reach the North Pole**
In 1909, American Robert Peary became the first to claim to have led a successful expedition to the North Pole. Many have since doubted his claims.

**First undisputed flight over the North Pole**
The brainchild of Roald Amundsen and Italian airship designer Umberto Nobile, the airship *Norge* made the first verified flight of any kind over the North Pole on May 12, 1926.

**First surface traveler known to have reached the North Pole**
On April 19, 1968, American Ralph Plaisted, using a snowmobile, completed a 43-day trip to the North Pole. It was the first verified overland trip to the pole.

The USS *Nautilus*'s trip under the polar ice cap was known as Operation Sunshine.

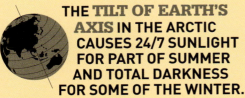

THE **TILT OF EARTH'S AXIS** IN THE ARCTIC CAUSES 24/7 SUNLIGHT FOR PART OF SUMMER AND TOTAL DARKNESS FOR SOME OF THE WINTER.

THE **NORTH STAR** SITS ABOVE THE NORTH POLE AND HAS LONG BEEN USED BY SAILORS TO HELP THEM NAVIGATE.

THE ARCTIC'S ICE HOLDS ABOUT 10 PERCENT OF THE WORLD'S FRESH WATER.

# ARCTIC RECORDS

The **Arctic region** is one of the world's most **inhospitable** environments and has proved one of the most **challenging** and **difficult** places on Earth for explorers.

**The North Pole is the world's most northerly point.** When you are standing there, any direction you point is south. No one actually lives at the North Pole, but expeditions to reach it started in the 19th century.

**First watercraft to reach the North Pole**
On August 3, 1958, the USS *Nautilus*, the world's first nuclear-powered submarine, became the first watercraft to reach the geographic North Pole. It went on to travel underneath the entire polar ice cap.

### FAST FACTS

**There is no land at the North Pole.** Instead, it is covered by floating ice, known as pack ice, between 9.8–13.1 ft (3–4 m) thick. Depending on the time of year, this pack ice covers an area of between 3.47–4.63 million sq miles (9–12 million sq km).

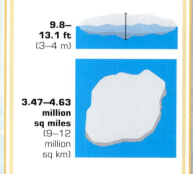

9.8–13.1 ft (3–4 m)

3.47–4.63 million sq miles (9–12 million sq km)

**Fastest trek to the North Pole**
In 1995, Russian Misha Malakhov (above, right) and Canadian Richard Weber took 123 days to trudge to the North Pole and back, dragging everything they needed behind them on 300 lb (136 kg) sleighs.

**THE ARCTIC IS HOME TO POLAR BEARS, WHICH ARE THE WORLD'S LARGEST LAND PREDATORS.**

**IN 1899, US EXPLORER ROBERT PEARY LOST EIGHT TOES TO FROSTBITE TRYING TO REACH THE NORTH POLE.**

ANTARCTICA HAS NO INDIGENOUS PEOPLE.

# ANTARCTIC RECORDS

**Antarctica** was the **last** of Earth's seven continents to be **discovered**. At the turn of the 20th century, the quest to become the first to reach the **South Pole** became the **greatest prize** in exploration.

**First to reach the South Pole**
Norwegian Roald Amundsen led a party of five to become the first to reach the South Pole. They arrived there on December 14, 1911, beating a British team, led by Robert F. Scott, by 35 days.

**First permanent base in Antarctica**
Ormond House—a meteorological (weather) observatory on Laurie Island (the second largest of the South Orkney Islands)—was established by the Scottish National Antarctic Expedition in 1903.

### AMUNDSEN VS. SCOTT

| Amundsen | | Scott |
|---|---|---|
| 5 men | | 17 men |
| 3 tons of supplies | | 1 ton of supplies |
| 52 huskies |  | 0 huskies |

Amundsen's mission to the South Pole was planned to perfection. An experienced polar explorer, he took exactly what was required. The graphic above shows the stark difference between the equipment taken by Amundsen and that taken by Scott.

**First to sight Antarctica**
On January 28, 1820, the crew of the Russian ship *Vostok*, captained by Admiral Fabian Gottlieb von Bellingshausen (above), became the first to sight Antarctica's coastline.

**ICEBERGS** ARE MUCH BIGGER UNDER THE SURFACE OF THE SEA THAN ABOVE IT.

THE BRITISH NAVAL OFFICER WHO MAPPED THE ANTARCTIC COAST IN 1839 FOUND AN ICE SHELF ABOUT THE SIZE OF **FRANCE**.

ANTARCTICA HAS TWO ACTIVE VOLCANOES: MOUNT EREBUS AND DECEPTION ISLAND.

**First flight over the South Pole**
On November 29, 1929, American Richard Byrd (above), along with pilot Bernt Balchen, co-pilot Harold June, and photographer Ashley McKinley, became the first person to fly over the South Pole.

**First overland crossing of Antarctica**
On March 2, 1958, members of the Commonwealth Trans-Antarctic Expedition, led by Englishman Vivien Fuchs (right) and Edmund Hillary (NZ, left), completed the first successful overland crossing of Antarctica. They covered 2,158 miles (3,473 km).

Emilio Marcos Palma of Argentina was the first person born on mainland Antarctica, in 1978.

**First all-women's team to reach the South Pole**
On January 14, 1993, four women of the American Women's Expedition (led by Ann Bancroft, above) became the first all-women's team to reach the South Pole. It took them 67 days to achieve the feat.

Antarctica has the highest average elevation of any continent in the world—7,545 ft (2,300 m). The South Pole itself sits on top of the Antarctic Plateau at a height of 9,301 ft (2,835 m).

 THE 1959 ANTARCTIC TREATY BANNED ALL MILITARY AND INDUSTRIAL ACTIVITIES ACROSS THE CONTINENT.

 ONLY ABOUT 0.4 PERCENT OF THE TOTAL SURFACE AREA OF ANTARCTICA IS WITHOUT SNOW AND ICE.

PARK RANGER ROY SULLIVAN WAS HIT BY LIGHTNING SEVEN TIMES—AND SURVIVED!

# I'M A SURVIVOR

Pushed to the **limits**, these people have all proved their **strength** and **stamina** by **staying alive** in some of the most **extreme conditions** and **environments** on Earth.

## Longest time ADRIFT AT SEA

**When a storm in October 1813** damaged Captain Oguri Jukichi's ship off the coast of Japan, he and two crewmates were adrift for 484 days. Only in March 1815 did another ship come to the rescue. Luckily, some of the ship's cargo was soybeans, which had kept them alive.

## Lowest body TEMPERATURE

**In 1999** Norwegian radiologist Anna Bågenholm survived the lowest adult body temperature ever recorded when she fell under ice while skiing. Her temperature dropped to 56.7°F (13.7°C)—a healthy body temperature is 98.6°F (37°C).

### FAST FACTS

**The "rule of three"** says people can survive for...

 **3 minutes** without air

 **3 hours** without shelter (unless in icy water)

 **3 days** without water (if sheltered from harsh environment)

 **3 weeks** without food (if you have water and shelter)

This is just a guide: a person may last three hours without shelter in freezing conditions, but not if they are wet, which makes hypothermia set in more quickly. In icy water, survival time may range from 15 minutes to around an hour.

**AFTER A 2023 PLANE CRASH, FOUR CHILDREN SURVIVED ON PLANTS FOR 40 DAYS IN THE AMAZONIAN RAINFOREST.**

**LOST IN THE SAHARA DESERT FOR 10 DAYS IN 1994, ATHLETE MAURO PROSPERI SURVIVED ON LIZARDS AND HIS OWN PEE.**

IN 1962, JOHANNES RELLEKE IN ZIMBABWE SURVIVED 2,443 BEE STINGS.

## Longest time TRAPPED UNDERGROUND

**When the San José copper-gold mine** in Chile collapsed in 2010, it left 33 miners underground. They remained trapped for a record-breaking 69 days until a rescue mission lifted them 2,257 ft (688 m) to safety.

## Most time on a DESERT ISLAND

**From 1704 to 1709, Alexander Selkirk** spent four years and four months cast away on an island off the coast of Chile. The British naval officer's experience inspired the famous novel *Robinson Crusoe* (1719) by Daniel Defoe.

## Longest time in the DESERT

**American Robert Bogucki** wandered in the Great Sandy Desert, Australia, on a spiritual quest for 43 days before being rescued in 1999. He was located by the crew of a TV company helicopter, which had been following the second search team.

**Not everyone on this page** is an accidental hero. While Captain Jukichi and the Chilean miners were simply going about their (very dangerous) jobs when disaster struck, Alexander Selkirk supposedly demanded to be put off his ship and onto his desert island.

A US HUNTER IN 1823 WAS SAVAGED BY A **BEAR** BUT SURVIVED AFTER STAGGERING 200 MILES (320 KM) TO SAFETY.

SERBIA'S VESNA VULOVIĆ FELL FROM A CRASHING PLANE, PLUNGING 33,000 FT (10,000 M) WITHOUT A PARACHUTE. SHE LIVED!

# Sporting prowess

When it comes to sports, only the best and the most dedicated make it to the very top of their game. Records are set and broken as champions blow away the competition to add their names to the sporting world's roll of honors.

**Brazil's captain, Cafu**, holds aloft the soccer World Cup trophy after his team's 2–0 victory over Germany in the 2002 final. Following tournament victories in 1958, 1962, 1970, and 1994, it was the country's fifth success in the competition—the most by any country in the tournament's history.

THE FIRST OLYMPIC GAMES WAS HELD AT OLYMPIA IN GREECE IN 776 BCE.

### FIRST CHAMPION

American James Connolly is credited as being the first modern champion at the Olympic Games. He won the opening event at the 1896 Games held in Athens, Greece—the triple jump.

**Most medals (male)**
American swimmer Michael Phelps is the runaway winner with 28 Olympic medals, including 23 golds. He won eight golds in Beijing, 2008—the most golds in a single Games.

**Most medals (female)**
Soviet (Russian) gymnast Larisa Latynina won a record-breaking 18 Olympic medals between 1956 and 1964.

Larisa Latynina's record for most medals stood for 48 years before Michael Phelps broke it.

Michael Phelps

Larisa Latynina

# OLYMPIC ACHIEVERS

All athletes **go for gold** at the **Olympics**, aiming to fulfill the motto of "**Faster, Higher, Stronger.**" But who is the **best of the best**?

AN **OLYMPIC GOLD MEDAL** IS ACTUALLY 92.5 PERCENT SILVER, COVERED WITH AROUND 0.2 OZ (6 G) OF PURE GOLD.

PARTICIPANTS AT THE **ANCIENT OLYMPIC GAMES** COMPETED NAKED. ONLY MEN WERE ALLOWED TO TAKE PART.

**WOMEN WERE FIRST ALLOWED TO TAKE PART IN THE OLYMPIC GAMES IN 1900.**

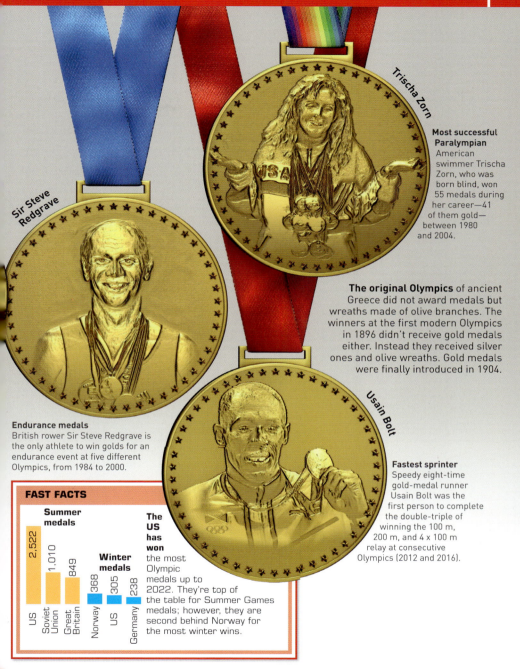

*Trischa Zorn*

**Most successful Paralympian**
American swimmer Trischa Zorn, who was born blind, won 55 medals during her career—41 of them gold—between 1980 and 2004.

The **original Olympics** of ancient Greece did not award medals but wreaths made of olive branches. The winners at the first modern Olympics in 1896 didn't receive gold medals either. Instead they received silver ones and olive wreaths. Gold medals were finally introduced in 1904.

*Sir Steve Redgrave*

**Endurance medals**
British rower Sir Steve Redgrave is the only athlete to win golds for an endurance event at five different Olympics, from 1984 to 2000.

*Usain Bolt*

**Fastest sprinter**
Speedy eight-time gold-medal runner Usain Bolt was the first person to complete the double-triple of winning the 100 m, 200 m, and 4 x 100 m relay at consecutive Olympics (2012 and 2016).

### FAST FACTS

**Summer medals**
- US: 2,522
- Soviet Union: 1,010
- Great Britain: 849

**Winter medals**
- Norway: 368
- US: 305
- Germany: 238

The US has won the most Olympic medals up to 2022. They're top of the table for Summer Games medals; however, they are second behind Norway for the most winter wins.

**AT BERLIN IN 1936, TWO JAPANESE POLE-VAULTERS WHO CAME JOINT SECOND WON HALF SILVER AND HALF BRONZE MEDALS!**

**THE OLYMPIC FLAME IS CARRIED BY RELAY RUNNERS ALL THE WAY FROM OLYMPIA IN GREECE TO THE HOST NATION.**

## OTHER GOAL-SCORING RECORDS

**Most goals scored at the World Cup:** 16—Miroslav Klose (Germany, 2002–2014).

**Most goals scored at a single World Cup:** 13—Just Fontaine (France, 1958).

**Most goals scored in a single World Cup match:** 5—Oleg Salenko (Russia) v Cameroon, 1994.

**Most goals scored in a World Cup final:** 3—Geoff Hurst (England), 1966, and Kylian Mbappé (France), 2022.

**Most goals scored in a career:** 1,468—Josef Bican (Austria) in 918 matches between 1931 and 1956.

**Most international goals:** 128—Cristiano Ronaldo (in 205 international matches for Portugal, 2003 onward).

**Most goals scored in a single international match:** 13—Archie Thompson (Australia) v American Samoa. Australia won the qualifying match for the 2002 World Cup 31–0.

**Most goals in a calendar year:** 91—Lionel Messi (for Barcelona and Argentina in 2012).

**Tom King's goal** was not enough to win the match, however. It ended in a 1–1 draw.

**Unusually, a goalkeeper scored** the longest goal in a competitive soccer match. On January 19, 2021, Tom King scored for Newport County against Cheltenham Town in the English Football League Two. His goal kick flew, bounced on the edge of the box, and went in. The length of the shot: 301.5 ft (91.9 m).

**CHINESE** DOCUMENTS FROM ABOUT 2500 BCE DESCRIBE PEOPLE KICKING OBJECTS AT MATERIAL STRETCHED BETWEEN TWO STICKS.

IN 1942, STEPHAN STANIS SCORED 16 GOALS IN ONE GAME FOR FRENCH TEAM RC LENS AGAINST AUBRY ASTURIES.

ABOUT 70 PERCENT OF THE WORLD'S SOCCER BALLS ARE MANUFACTURED IN PAKISTAN.

# GOAL!!!

Soccer is the **world's most popular sport**. Many thousands of matches have been played in every corner of the globe, but what is the **longest goal ever scored** in an official match?

**The record-breaking** shot was helped by a strong following wind.

The record for the **most goals scored by a goalkeeper is 131, by Brazil's Rogério Ceni.**

THE 2005 NAMIBIAN CUP WAS DECIDED BY A RECORD-BREAKING **48 PENALTY KICKS.** KK PALACE BEAT THE CIVICS 17–16.

IN 2011, WHEN CLUB ATLÉTICO CLAYPOLE PLAYED VICTORIANO ARENAS (ARGENTINA), A RECORD 36 PEOPLE WERE **SENT OFF!**

**FIFA AIMS TO HAVE 60 MILLION WOMEN PLAYING SOCCER BY 2026.**

**A veteran of four World Cups,** Canada's Christine Sinclair has scored 190 goals in 328 games since her debut in 2000.

**A World Cup winner** in 2015 with the US, Abby Wambach scored 184 goals in 255 matches between 2001 and 2015.

**The most famous player** in women's soccer at the turn of the 21st century, Mia Hamm scored 158 goals in 276 matches for the US between 1987 and 2004.

**Two-time World Cup winner** for the US, Carli Lloyd scored 134 goals in 316 games from 2005 to 2021.

Christine Sinclair — 190
Abby Wambach — 184
Mia Hamm — 158
Carli Lloyd — 134

**Carli Lloyd is the only woman to score a hat-trick in a World Cup final.**

 **THE FIRST PUBLIC WOMEN'S GAME TOOK PLACE IN 1895 IN LONDON. NORTH BEAT SOUTH 7-1.**

 **IN 1921, THE FOOTBALL ASSOCIATION BANNED WOMEN'S SOCCER,** CLAIMING IT WAS "QUITE UNSUITABLE FOR FEMALES."

BRAZIL'S MIRAILDES MACIEL MOTA PLAYED IN THE MOST WORLD CUPS: SEVEN!

# HOT SHOTS

The **first** official women's international was played in **1971**—99 years after the first men's match. But that has not stopped **women soccer players** from producing some **record-breaking** performances.

**Jordanian forward** Maysa Jbarah has scored 133 goals in 129 matches for Jordan since her debut in 2005.

Maysa Jbarah

133

**Eighteen women** have scored more than 100 goals in women's international soccer. Here are the top five.

### WORLD CUP GOAL-SCORING RECORDS

**Leading goalscorer:** Marta (Brazil, below)—17 goals in six tournament appearances between 2003 and 2023.

**Most goals scored in a single tournament:** 10—Michelle Akers (US) in 1991.

**Most goals in a single match:** 5—Michelle Akers (US) v Chinese Taipei on November 24, 1991.

**Fastest hat-trick:** 5 minutes—Fabienne Humm (Switzerland) against Ecuador on June 12, 2015.

**Fastest goal from kick-off:** 30 seconds—Lena Videkull (Sweden) against Japan on November 19, 1991.

**Youngest goal-scorer:** Elena Danilova (Russia) was 16 years 107 days old when she scored against Germany on October 2, 2003.

**Oldest goal-scorer:** Formiga (Brazil) was 37 years 98 days old when she scored against South Korea on June 9, 2015.

Marta

THE RECORD CROWD FOR A WOMEN'S MATCH WAS **91,648** AT BARCELONA'S NOU CAMP STADIUM, SPAIN, IN 2022.

THE FIRST FIFA WOMEN'S **WORLD CUP** TOURNAMENT IN 1991 FEATURED 12 TEAMS. IN 2023, IT FEATURED 32.

THE CINCINNATI RED STOCKINGS BECAME THE FIRST PROFESSIONAL CLUB IN 1869.

# HOME-RUN HEROICS

**Baseball** is a sport that is particularly associated with **numbers**, but perhaps the best-known number of all is **73**—the record for the highest number of **home runs** hit in a **single season**.

### PERFECT PITCHING

**Most complete games in an MLB career:** 749—Cy Young (between 1890 and 1911). A complete game is when a pitcher throws an entire game without a relief pitcher.

**Most no-hitters in a career:** 7—Nolan Ryan (between 1966 and 1993). A no-hitter is a game in which a team was not able to get a single player onto first base.

**Most career shutouts:** 110—Walter Johnson (between 1907 and 1927). A shutout is when a pitcher pitches a complete game and does not allow the opposing team to score a run.

**Most career strikeouts:** 5,714—Nolan Ryan (between 1966 and 1993). A strikeout is when a batter records three strikes at a single at bat.

**Cal Ripken Jr.** played a record **2,632 consecutive games** between 1982 and 1999.

AMERICAN PITCHER **EDWIN JACKSON** MADE HISTORY IN 2019 AS THE FIRST PERSON TO PLAY FOR 14 MAJOR LEAGUE TEAMS.

TWO NEW YORK YANKEES MANAGERS SHARE THE RECORD FOR THE MOST **WORLD SERIES** WINS—SEVEN EACH.

WITH 56,000 SEATS, LA'S DODGER STADIUM IS THE BIGGEST BASEBALL ARENA.

**On October 5, 2001**, at Pacific Bell Park, the San Francisco Giants' Barry Bonds hit his 71st home run of the season to break Mark McGwire's single-season home-run record. He went on to hit 73. This illustration shows where and how far he hit each of those home runs.

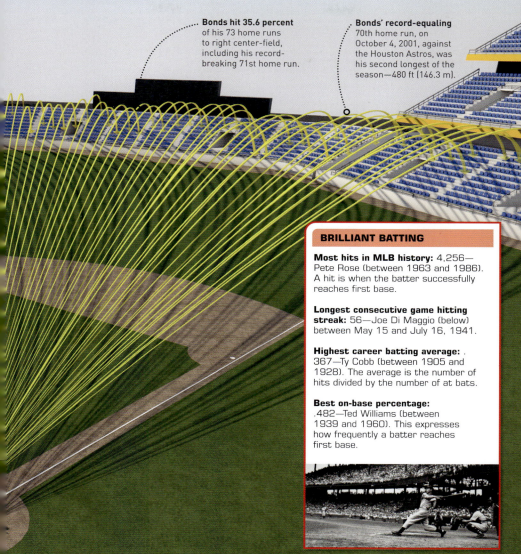

**Bonds hit 35.6 percent** of his 73 home runs to right center-field, including his record-breaking 71st home run.

**Bonds' record-equaling** 70th home run, on October 4, 2001, against the Houston Astros, was his second longest of the season—480 ft (146.3 m).

### BRILLIANT BATTING

**Most hits in MLB history:** 4,256—Pete Rose (between 1963 and 1986). A hit is when the batter successfully reaches first base.

**Longest consecutive game hitting streak:** 56—Joe Di Maggio (below) between May 15 and July 16, 1941.

**Highest career batting average:** .367—Ty Cobb (between 1905 and 1928). The average is the number of hits divided by the number of at bats.

**Best on-base percentage:** .482—Ted Williams (between 1939 and 1960). This expresses how frequently a batter reaches first base.

BABE RUTH (1935), HANK AARON (1976), AND BARRY BONDS (2007) ALL HIT OVER 700 HOME RUNS IN PRO BASEBALL.

OPENED IN 1877, LABATT PARK IN LONDON, CANADA, IS THE OLDEST IN-USE BASEBALL STADIUM.

**FORMULA 1 DRIVERS NEED AN F1 "SUPER LICENSE" TO COMPETE.**

**Motorsport is hugely popular** in all corners of the world, but of the sport's big four categories—Formula One, Indycar, NASCAR, and MotoGP—which has produced the fastest vehicle?

**Formula One**
Most championships:
7—Michael Schumacher (Germany, above) and Lewis Hamilton (UK)
Most race wins:
103—Lewis Hamilton
Most pole positions:
104—Lewis Hamilton
Most constructors' championships:
16—Ferrari

**Indycar**
Most championships:
7—A. J. Foyt (US, above)
Most race wins:
67—A. J. Foyt (US)
Most pole positions:
68—Will Power (Australia)
Most constructors' championships:
231—Team Penske (most race wins)

**MotoGP**
Most championships:
8—Giacomo Agostini (Italy)
Most race wins:
89—Valentino Rossi (Italy, above)
Most pole positions:
62—Marc Márquez (Spain)
Most constructors' championships:
25—Honda

**NASCAR**
Most championships:
7—Richard Petty (above), Dale Earnhardt Jr., Jimmie Johnson
Most race wins:
200—Richard Petty
Most pole positions:
123—Richard Petty
Most constructors' championships:
42—Chevrolet

**234.878 mph (378 km/h)**
Formula 1
Valterri Bottas (Finland) hit this jaw-dropping speed at the 2016 Mexican Grand Prix.

**FORMULA 1 CARS** CAN ACCELERATE FROM 0 TO 100 MPH (160 KM/H) IN FOUR SECONDS, AND BRAKE BACK DOWN TO ZERO IN FOUR SECONDS.

**FORMULA 1 MECHANICS** CAN CHANGE ALL FOUR TIRES IN THREE SECONDS DURING RACES.

A FORMULA 1 RACING CAR HAS AROUND 80,000 SEPARATE COMPONENTS.

# KINGS OF
# THE ROAD

People have **raced** on two wheels and on four for as long as **motorcycles and cars** have been around, but who have proved the true **masters of motorsport**?

NASCAR's **Richard Petty** celebrated a world-record 200 race wins during his career.

**212.809 mph (342.483 km/h)**
NASCAR
Bill Elliott (US) recorded NASCAR's fastest-ever speed at Talladega, Alabama, on April 30, 1987.

**227.4 mph (366.1 km/h)**
MotoGP
Brad Binder (South Africa) became MotoGP's fastest at Mugello, Italy, in 2023.

**237.498 mph (382.216 km/h)**
Indycar
Arie Luyendyk (Netherlands) clocked this speed in qualifying for the 1996 Indy 500 at Indianapolis, Indiana.

 INDY 500 RACE WINNERS HAVE CELEBRATED BY DRINKING **MILK** EVER SINCE LOUIS MEYER FIRST DOWNED A BOTTLE AFTER HIS 1936 WIN.

 TWENTY-NINE NATIONALITIES HAVE WON THE MOTORCYCLE GRAND PRIX. ITALY IS IN POLE POSITION, HAVING BAGGED **811** VICTORIES.

GOLF IS THE ONLY SPORT TO HAVE BEEN PLAYED ON THE MOON.

# Sports data

## FANTASTIC SOCCER RECORDS

### MOST WORLD CUP WINS

**5** **BRAZIL** (1958, 1962, 1970, 1994, 2002)

**4** **GERMANY** (1954, 1974, 1990, 2014)
**ITALY** (1934, 1938, 1982, 2006)

**3** **ARGENTINA** (1978, 1986, 2022)

**2** **FRANCE** (1998, 2018)
**URUGUAY** (1930, 1950)

**1** **ENGLAND** (1966)
**SPAIN** (2010)

### MOST WOMEN'S WORLD CUP WINS

**4** **USA** (1991, 1999, 2015, 2019)

**2** **GERMANY** (2003, 2007)

**1** **NORWAY** (1995)
**JAPAN** (2011)
**SPAIN** (2023)

## MOST SUCCESSFUL SOCCER TEAMS

- **MOST SUCCESSFUL TEAMS AT THE EUROPEAN CHAMPIONSHIPS:** Germany (1972, 1980, 1996) and Spain (1964, 2008, 2012) have both won the title on three occasions.

- **MOST SUCCESSFUL TEAM AT THE COPA AMERICA:** Uruguay and Argentina have both claimed the title on 15 occasions.

- **MOST SUCCESSFUL TEAM IN THE CHAMPIONS LEAGUE:** Real Madrid (Spain) has won the tournament on 14 occasions, including five straight wins between 1956 and 1960. Milan (Italy) lies second on the list with seven victories.

- **MOST SUCCESSFUL TEAM IN THE COPA LIBERTADORES:** Independiente (Argentina) is the tournament's most successful team, with seven victories. Compatriots Boca Juniors is second on the list with six wins.

- **MOST SUCCESSFUL DOMESTIC TEAM IN HISTORY:** Rangers (Scotland) and Al Ahly (Egypt) have both won 55 titles.

## HIGHEST SCORE

The **highest score** in a competitive soccer match is **149–0**, in a match between **SO l'Emyrne** and **AS Adema** in Madagascar on October 31, 2002. Enraged by the performance of the officials in their previous match, SO l'Emyrne scored 149 own-goals!

IN 2020, A RECORD-BREAKING **TABLE TENNIS** RALLY BETWEEN TWO AUSTRALIANS LASTED 11 HOURS 50 MINUTES.

IN 2021, BRITISH **SNOOKER PLAYER JAMES SILVERWOOD** CLEARED ALL THE COLORED BALLS IN ONLY 17 SECONDS.

THE FASTEST SPEED FOR A BOWLED CRICKET BALL EXCEEDED 100 MPH (160 KM/H).

## ICE HOCKEY GREAT

**Wayne Gretzky,** dubbed **the Great One,** is the most **famous player in NHL history.** He holds **numerous all-time records.** Here are the best of them:

**MOST POINTS IN A SINGLE SEASON:** 215 IN 1985–1986
**MOST POINTS IN A CAREER:** 2,857 POINTS
**MOST REGULAR SEASON POINTS PER GAME:** 1.921
**MOST REGULAR SEASON GOALS:** 894
**MOST REGULAR SEASON ASSISTS:** 1,963
**MOST PLAYOFF POINTS:** 382

## HOOP HEROICS — BASKETBALL

**MOST CONSECUTIVE WINS IN AN NBA SEASON:** 33—LA Lakers in the 1971–1972 season (the second-best mark in NBA history is 28 consecutive wins).

**NBA SINGLE-GAME SCORING RECORD:** 100 points—Wilt Chamberlain, for the Philadelphia Warriors versus the New York Knicks on March 2, 1962. *The closest anyone has gotten to the record since is 81 points—Kobe Bryant, for the LA Lakers against the Toronto Raptors on January 22, 2006.*

**MOST CONSECUTIVE NBA TITLES:** 8—Boston Celtics between 1959 and 1966.

**MOST ASSISTS IN AN NBA CAREER:** 15,806—John Stockton *(the closest active player is Chris Paul, who is more than 6,000 assists behind).*

**MOST CAREER NBA POINTS:** 39,797—LeBron James, from 2003 onward.

**MOST CONSECUTIVE NBA GAMES WITH 10 POINTS OR MORE:** 1,125—Lebron James, from 2007 to January 2023 (and still counting).

## GRIDIRON GREATS — FOOTBALL

**BIGGEST VICTORY:** Georgia Tech beat Cumberland University by the staggering margin of 222–0 in a college match on October 7, 1916.

**MOST CONSECUTIVE NFL GAMES PLAYED:** 297—Brett Favre. He played in every consecutive game for 19 seasons between 1992 and 2010, playing for three teams—Green Bay Packers, New York Jets, and Minnesota Vikings.

**THE LONGEST PLAY IN NFL HISTORY:** 109.88 yards—Antonio Cromartie playing for San Diego Chargers against Minnesota Vikings on November 4, 2007. He returned a missed field goal for a touchdown.

**MOST CAREER RECEIVING YARDS:** 22,895 yards—Jerry Rice (between 1985 and 2004). Larry Fitzgerald, who played in the NFL between 2004 and 2020, is in second place.

**MOST CAREER RECEPTIONS:** 1,549—Jerry Rice.

**MOST CAREER RUSHING YARDS:** 18,355—Emmitt Smith.

**MOST CONSECUTIVE GAMES WITH A TOUCHDOWN PASS:** 54—Drew Brees (set between 2009 and 2012 while playing for New Orleans Saints).

**MOST PASSING TOUCHDOWNS (CAREER):** 649—Tom Brady (between 2000 and 2023).

**MOST SUPER BOWL WINS:** 6—Pittsburgh Steelers (1975, 1976, 1979, 1980, 2006, 2009). 6—New England Patriots (2002, 2004, 2005, 2015, 2017, 2019).

THE LONGEST **TENNIS MATCH** WAS AT WIMBLEDON IN 2010. AFTER 11 HOURS 5 MINUTES, JOHN ISNER BEAT NICOLAS MAHUT.

THE BIGGEST WIN IN INTERNATIONAL **RUGBY** WAS 142–0 (AUSTRALIA–NAMIBIA) IN 2003.

LONG JUMP FROM A STANDING START WAS AN OLYMPIC EVENT UNTIL 1912.

Top-class **long jumpers** reach a **speed of 33 ft/s (10 m/s)** on the runway.

**Athletes try to reach** the ideal speed before takeoff.

### GIANT LEAP

It may no longer be the world record, but Bob Beamon's jump at the 1968 Olympics is the most famous long jump in history. The American's leap of 29.2 ft (8.90 m) broke the existing world record by 21.7 in (55 cm).

**The current long jump world record** was set by US athlete Mike Powell at the 1991 World Championships in Tokyo, Japan—29.36 ft (8.95 m). That's the equivalent of jumping farther than the length of two original-style Volkswagen Beetles.

**LONG JUMP** WAS ONE OF THE EVENTS IN THE PENTATHLON ("FIVE COMPETITION") AT THE ANCIENT OLYMPICS.

ANCIENT GREEK LONG JUMPERS CARRIED WEIGHTS, CALLED **HALTERE** TO CREATE GREATE MOMENTUM.

WOMEN BEGAN COMPETING IN LONG JUMP ONLY AT THE 1948 OLYMPICS.

# LONGEST JUMP

The **long jump** is a track-and-field event that requires speed, technique, and strength to **leap as far as possible** from a fixed point. It has been contested at **every Olympics** since 1896.

**Once in the air,** the athlete will move his arms and legs forward and will try to hang in the air. This is known as the "hitch-kick."

**On landing,** the athlete will try to propel his body beyond the initial landing point to increase the distance of his jump.

**Mike Powell's record** has now stood for over 30 years—it is the third-longest-standing world record in athletics.

### HISTORIC JUMPS

- ⑤ 24.7 ft (7.52 m)—Galina Chistyakova (Russia, 1988)
  *The only woman in history to jump more than 24.6 ft (7.5 m).*
- ④ 24.96 ft (7.61 m)—Peter O'Connor (Ireland, 1901)
  *First record ratified by International Association of Athletics Federation.*
- ③ 26.67 ft (8.13 m)—Jesse Owens (US, 1935)
  *First jump in history to exceed 26.24 ft (8 m).*
- ② 29.2 ft (8.90 m)—Bob Beamon (US, 1968)
  *Beamon's leap shattered the world record by 21.7 in (55 cm).*
- ① 29.36 ft (8.95 m)—Mike Powell (US, 1991)
  *Powell beat Bob Beamon's world-record leap by 2 in (5 cm).*

**17** HISTORIC GREEK RECORDS SUGGEST PHAYLLOS OF KRATON JUMPED **17 M** (55 FT) AND LANDED BEYOND THE SAND PIT!

MODERN LONG JUMPERS CAN WEAR **SPIKED SHOES** BUT THE SOLES MUST NOT EXCEED 13 MM (0.5 IN) IN THICKNESS.

POLE VAULTERS TAKE A RUN-UP OF 130 FT (40 M) BEFORE TAKING OFF.

### WORLD RECORDS

These are the current men's and women's world records.

**1** MEN'S—20.4 ft (6.23 m)
Armand Duplantis (2023)

**2** WOMEN'S—16.6 ft (5.06 m)
Yelena Isinbayeva (2009)

The vaulter prepares for the **"fly away,"** the easiest part of the jump. He will push off the top of the pole and rotate his body in an attempt to clear the bar.

Known as the **"swing up,"** the vaulter swings his legs up and starts to move his arms toward his hips.

The faster the vaulter can **run** down the runway, and the better he can execute the takeoff, the more the pole will bend. This will help the vaulter achieve a greater height.

**US** vaulters won **every pole-vault gold medal** at the Olympics between 1896 and 1968.

### ARMAND DUPLANTIS

On September 17, 2023, Sweden's Armand Duplantis broke Renaud Lavillenie's world record, clearing an astonishing 20.4 ft (6.23 m) in Eugene, Oregon. Duplantis is both Olympic and two-time outdoor world pole vaulting champion.

Athletes run up and plant **the pole** in a hole in the ground called a "box." Flexible poles, made of carbon fiber or fiberglass, were introduced in the 1950s, making it easier for vaulters to clear greater heights.

PAINTINGS FROM ANCIENT GREECE SHOW PEOPLE USING **SPEARLIKE** POLES TO CLEAR OBJECTS IN ABOUT 500 BCE.

IN THE PAST, THE POLES WERE HANDCRAFTED FROM WOOD BEFORE BEING REPLACED BY LIGHTER **BAMBOO**.

IN 2012, POLE VAULTER DAVID W. SLOVENSKI CLEARED 10 FT (3 M) ON A UNICYCLE!

# RAISING THE BAR

The pole vault is a **track-and-field event** in athletics in which vaulters use a **long, long, flexible pole to help them spring over a bar**.

**The current men's world record**—20.4 ft (6.23 m)—is greater than the height of an average giraffe (19.7 ft/6 m).

**After an attempt to clear the bar**, the vaulter starts a long descent to the ground. A crash mat softens the impact of the landing.

**The pole vault** has been a full-medal event at the Olympics since 1896 for men and since 2000 for women. Vaulters have three attempts to clear a height or a combination of heights. If they fail to do so, they are eliminated from the competition.

### YELENA ISINBAYEVA

Russia's Yelena Isinbayeva is the current women's world-record holder in the pole vault. A two-time Olympic gold medalist (in 2004 and 2008), she achieved her history-making leap of 16.6 ft (5.06 m) in Zurich, Switzerland, on August 28, 2009.

**MODERN METAL AND FIBERGLASS POLES LET POLE VAULTERS GO TWICE AS HIGH AS EARLY OLYMPIANS.**

IN 2012, AT AGE 90, WILLIAM BELL SET A NEW WORLD RECORD IN HIS AGE GROUP OF 7.2 FT (2.2 M).

ATHLETES FROM THE US HAVE WON THE MOST 100 METERS OLYMPIC GOLDS.

**The 100 m world record** is the ultimate prize for a sprinter. This illustration shows some of history's most memorable 100 m runs. It compares where the athletes would have been on the track when the current men's and women's world record holders crossed the finish line.

**11.4 seconds**
On October 4, 1952, Australian Marjorie Jackson became the first woman to run the 100 m in under 11.5 seconds.

**11.01 seconds**
West German Annegret Richter ran 11.01 seconds in the 100 m final at the 1976 Olympics in Canada.

**11.04 seconds**
West German Inge Helten broke the world record on June 13, 1976, and held it for 42 days.

**11.07 seconds**
Wyomia Tyus (US) broke the world record in the women's 100 m final at the 1968 Olympics in Mexico.

91 m  92 m  93 m  94 m  95 m

# 100-METER
## MARVELS

The world's **speediest sprinters** enter the 100-meter race. Winners are crowned the **fastest people on Earth**.

**Usain Bolt is the only athlete to win three successive Olympic 100 m titles.**

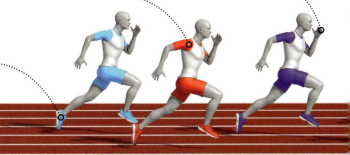

**10.2 seconds**
Jesse Owens (US) ran 10.2 seconds on June 20, 1936. The time would not be bettered for 20 years.

**10.1 seconds**
Willie Williams (US) clocked 10.1 seconds on August 3, 1956.

**10.3 seconds**
On August 9, 1930, Percy Williams (Canada) became the first man to run the 100 m under 10.4 seconds.

91 m  92 m  93 m  94 m  95 m

**BRITISH SPRINTER LINFORD CHRISTIE BECAME THE OLDEST 100 METERS OLYMPIC CHAMPION IN 1992, AT AGE 32.**

**AROUND 200 NATIONS TAKE PART IN THE OLYMPICS; ONLY 19 HAVE WON ANY MEDAL IN THE 100 METERS.**

THE 100 METERS WAS FIRST INCLUDED IN THE ATHENS OLYMPIC GAMES IN 1896.

**10.88 seconds**
On July 1, 1977, East German Marlies Oelsner produced the first electronically timed sub-11-second run.

**10.81 seconds**
Oelsner broke her own world record on June 8, 1983, but it lasted for only 25 days.

**10.79 seconds**
Evelyn Ashford (US) broke Oelsner's record on July 3, 1983, and became the first woman to run under 10.8 seconds.

**10.76 seconds**
Ashford bettered her own world record in Zurich, Switzerland, on August 22, 1984.

**10.49 seconds**
Florence Griffith-Joyner (US) smashed Ashford's world record by 0.3 seconds on July 16, 1988.

96 m    97 m    98 m    99 m    100 m

### FASTEST WOMAN

American Florence Griffith-Joyner has the fastest female feet in history, holding both the 100 m and 200 m world records. In 1988, Flo-Jo set a new 100 m record of 10.49 seconds.

### FASTEST MAN

Jamaican Usain Bolt is the fastest man ever in the 100 m and 200 m. Nicknamed "Lightning Bolt," he made history by running the 100 m in 9.58 seconds at the World Championships in Berlin in 2009.

**9.95 seconds**
Jim Hines (US) ran the first sub-10-second 100 m, in June 1968.

**9.93 seconds**
Calvin Smith (US) finally broke Jim Hines's record on July 3, 1983.

**9.86 seconds**
Carl Lewis (US) twice equaled Smith's record and finally broke it on August 25, 1991.

**9.79 seconds**
In June 1999, Maurice Greene (US) beat the 9.8-second mark for the first time.

**9.69 seconds**
Usain Bolt (Jamaica) broke his own world record at the 2008 Olympics in Beijing, China.

**9.58 seconds**
Usain Bolt set the current world record mark at the 2009 World Championships in Berlin, Germany.

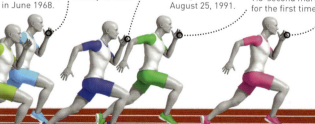

6 m    97 m    98 m    99 m    100 m

**ON THE NIGHT OF SPEED** IN 1968, JIM HINES, CHARLES GREENE, AND RONNIE RAY SMITH ALL RAN UNDER 10 SECONDS.

JUSTIN GATLIN OF THE US RAN AN AMAZING **9.45** SECONDS IN 2016, BUT HE USED WIND MACHINES, IN A STUNT FILMED FOR TV.

## LIGHTNING BOLT

**Usain Bolt is the fastest man on the planet.** The Jamaican has run the three fastest-ever times in the 100 m and is the current 200 m world record holder. He is also the only man in history to win the 100 m–200 m double at three consecutive Olympics (in 2008, 2012, and 2016).

MANY TRACK-AND-FIELD EVENTS FEATURED AT THE ANCIENT OLYMPIC GAMES.

# Amazing athletes

THESE ARE THE CURRENT **WORLD RECORD HOLDERS** FOR MAJOR EVENTS IN ATHLETICS:

## MEN'S FIELD EVENTS

| EVENT | RECORD | ATHLETE (COUNTRY) | LOCATION | DATE |
|---|---|---|---|---|
| HIGH JUMP | 2.45 M | JAVIER SOTOMAYOR (CUBA) | SALAMANCA, SPAIN | JULY 27, 1993 |
| POLE VAULT | 6.23 M | ARMAND DUPLANTIS (SWEDEN) | EUGENE, OREGON, US | SEPTEMBER 17, 2023 |
| LONG JUMP | 8.95 M | MIKE POWELL (US) | TOKYO, JAPAN | AUGUST 30, 1991 |
| TRIPLE JUMP | 18.29 M | JONATHAN EDWARDS (GB) | GOTHENBURG, SWEDEN | AUGUST 7, 1995 |
| SHOT PUT | 23.56 M | RYAN CROUSER (US) | LOS ANGELES, CA, US | MAY 23, 2023 |
| DISCUS THROW | 74.08 M | JÜRGEN SCHULT (EAST GERMANY) | NEUBRANDENBURG, EAST GERMANY | JUNE 6, 1986 |
| HAMMER THROW | 86.74 M | YURIY SEDYKH (RUSSIA) | STUTTGART, GERMANY | AUGUST 30, 1986 |
| JAVELIN THROW | 98.48 M | JAN ZELEZNY (CZECH REPUBLIC) | JENA, GERMANY | MAY 25, 1996 |
| DECATHLON | 9,126 PTS | KEVIN MAYER (FRANCE) | TALENCE, FRANCE | SEPTEMBER 16, 2018 |

## WOMEN'S FIELD EVENTS

| EVENT | RECORD | ATHLETE (COUNTRY) | LOCATION | DATE |
|---|---|---|---|---|
| HIGH JUMP | 2.09 M | STEFKA KOSTADINOVA (BULGARIA) | ROME, ITALY | AUGUST 30, 1987 |
| POLE VAULT | 5.06 M | YELENA ISINBAYEVA (RUSSIA) | ZURICH, SWITZERLAND | AUGUST 28, 2009 |
| LONG JUMP | 7.52 M | GALINA CHISTYAKOVA (USSR) | LENINGRAD, USSR | JUNE 11, 1988 |
| TRIPLE JUMP | 15.74 M | YULIMAR ROJAS (VENEZUELA) | BELGRADE, SERBIA | MARCH 20, 2022 |
| SHOT PUT | 22.63 M | NATALYA LISOVSKAYA (USSR) | MOSCOW, RUSSIA | JUNE 7, 1987 |
| DISCUS THROW | 76.80 M | GABRIELE REINSCH (EAST GERMANY) | NEUBRANDENBURG, EAST GERMANY | JULY 9, 1988 |
| HAMMER THROW | 82.98 M | ANITA WLODARCZYK (POLAND) | WARSAW, POLAND | AUGUST 28, 2016 |
| JAVELIN THROW | 72.28 M | BARBORA SPOTAKOVA (CZECH REPUBLIC) | STUTTGART, GERMANY | SEPTEMBER 13, 2008 |
| HEPTATHLON | 7,291 PTS | JACKIE JOYNER-KERSEE (US) | SEOUL, SOUTH KOREA | SEPTEMBER 24, 1988 |

IN 1936, GODFREY AND AUDREY BROWN BECAME THE FIRST SIBLINGS TO WIN TRACK AND FIELD MEDALS AT THE SAME OLYMPICS.

DICK FOSBURY WON HIGH JUMP GOLD AT THE 1968 OLYMPICS USING HIS "BACK FIRST" **FOSBURY FLOP** TECHNIQUE!

BOTH THE HAMMER AND THE SHOT PUT WEIGH 16 LB (7 KG).

## MEN'S TRACK EVENTS

| EVENT | RECORD | ATHLETE (COUNTRY) | LOCATION | DATE |
|---|---|---|---|---|
| 100 M | 9.58S | USAIN BOLT (JAMAICA) | BERLIN, GERMANY | AUGUST 16, 2009 |
| 200 M | 19.19S | USAIN BOLT (JAMAICA) | BERLIN, GERMANY | AUGUST 20, 2009 |
| 400 M | 43.03S | WAYDE VAN NIEKERK (SOUTH AFRICA) | RIO DE JANEIRO, BRAZIL | AUGUST 14, 2016 |
| 800 M | 1:40.91 | DAVID RUSHIDA (KENYA) | LONDON, ENGLAND | AUGUST 9, 2012 |
| 1,500 M | 3:26.00 | HICHAM EL GUERROUJ (MOROCCO) | ROME, ITALY | JULY 14, 1998 |
| 5,000 M | 12:35.36 | JOSHUA CHEPTEGEI (UGANDA) | MONACO | AUGUST 14, 2020 |
| 10,000 M | 26:11.00 | JOSHUA CHEPTEGEI (UGANDA) | VALENCIA, SPAIN | OCTOBER 7, 2020 |
| MARATHON | 2:00:35 | KELVIN KIPTUM (KENYA) | CHICAGO, ILLINOIS, US | OCTOBER 8, 2023 |
| 110 M HURDLES | 12.72S | SASHA ZHOYA (FRANCE) | NAIROBI, KENYA | AUGUST 21, 2021 |
| 400 M HURDLES | 45.94S | KARSTEN WARHOLM (NORWAY) | TOKYO, JAPAN | AUGUST 3, 2021 |
| 4 X 100 RELAY | 36.84S | JAMAICA | LONDON, ENGLAND | AUGUST 11, 2012 |
| 4 X 400 RELAY | 2:54.29 | USA | STUTTGART, GERMANY | AUGUST 22, 1993 |

## WOMEN'S TRACK EVENTS

| EVENT | RECORD | ATHLETE (COUNTRY) | LOCATION | DATE |
|---|---|---|---|---|
| 100 M | 10.49S | FLORENCE GRIFFITH-JOYNER (US) | INDIANAPOLIS, INDIANA, US | JULY 16, 1988 |
| 200 M | 21.34S | FLORENCE GRIFFITH-JOYNER (US) | SEOUL, SOUTH KOREA | SEPTEMBER 29, 1988 |
| 400 M | 47.60S | MARITA KOCH (EAST GERMANY) | CANBERRA, AUSTRALIA | OCTOBER 6, 1985 |
| 800 M | 1:53.28 | JARMILA KRATOCHVILOVA (CZECHOSLOVAKIA) | MUNICH, GERMANY | JULY 26, 1983 |
| 1,500 M | 3:49.11 | FAITH KIPYEGON (KENYA) | FLORENCE, ITALY | JUNE 2, 2023 |
| 5,000 M | 14:00.21 | GUDAF TSEGAY (ETHIOPIA) | OREGON, US | SEPTEMBER 17, 2023 |
| 10,000 M | 29:01.03 | LETESENBET GIDEY (ETHIOPIA) | HENGELO, NETHERLANDS | JUNE 8, 2021 |
| MARATHON | 2:11.53 | TIGST ASSEFA (ETHIOPIA) | BERLIN, GERMANY | SEPTEMBER 24, 2023 |
| 100 M HURDLES | 12.10S | TOBI AMUSAN (NIGERIA) | EUGENE, OREGON, US | JULY 24, 2022 |
| 400 M HURDLES | 50.68S | SYDNEY MCLAUGHLIN (US) | EUGENE, OREGON, US | JULY 22, 2022 |
| 4 X 100 RELAY | 40.82S | USA | LONDON, ENGLAND | AUGUST 10, 2012 |
| 4 X 400 RELAY | 3:15.17 | USSR | SEOUL, SOUTH KOREA | OCTOBER 1, 1988 |

EACH **BARRIER** IN THE 400 M HURDLES RACE IS 36 IN (91.4 CM) FOR MEN AND 30 IN (76.3 CM) FOR WOMEN.

**1970s**

WOMEN WERE BANNED FROM THE MARATHON UNTIL THE 1970s. IT WAS SAID THEY WERE TOO WEAK TO RUN THE DISTANCE.

AT THE 1980 OLYMPICS, COMANECI WON TWO MORE GYMNASTICS GOLDS.

**A rule passed after 1976** required an Olympian to be at least 16 years old. This means Comăneci's record for being the youngest-ever all-around gymnastics champion will never be beaten.

### IMPERFECT SCOREBOARD

The organizers of the 1976 Olympics did not believe anyone could score 10, so they made room for only three digits on the scoreboard. When Comăneci's score was revealed to the crowd, it showed only 1.00.

**Having already been awarded** the Olympic Games' first-ever perfect 10 for her routine on the parallel bars, 14-year-old Nadia Comăneci went on to receive six more 10s, including one for this performance on the balance beam.

FOLLOWING HER SUCCESS AT THE 1976 OLYMPICS, COMĂNECI WAS NAMED A NATIONAL HERO BY THE PRESIDENT OF **ROMANIA**.

THE SONG PLAYED DURING COMĂNECI'S FLOOR EXERCISE BECAME A BIG HIT AND WON A **GRAMMY AWARD** IN 1977.

NADIA COMANECI RETIRED FROM COMPETITIVE GYMNASTICS IN 1984, AT AGE 23.

# PERFECT 10

In 1976, **Romanian gymnast Nadia Comăneci** became the first person to achieve a **perfect 10** at an Olympics gymnastics event. But this was only the first of **seven standout performances** at the 1976 Games in Montreal, Canada, which made **sporting history**.

**Comăneci is the Olympics' youngest-ever all-around gymnastics champion.**

**Comăneci's balance beam was flawless**, as she dazzled the crowd with graceful poses, fluid movements, and unmatched steadiness.

**NADIA COMĂNECI WAS INDUCTED INTO THE INTERNATIONAL GYMNASTICS HALL OF FAME IN 1993.**

**COMĂNECI AND HER HUSBAND, FORMER USA GYMNAST BART CONNER, NOW RUN A SCHOOL FOR YOUNG GYMNASTS.**

# Feats of engineering

All around us is proof of what can be achieved when visionary designs are brought to life by hard work. Time-saving transportation to cross continents, stunning structures to redefine skylines, and marvelous machines to revolutionize the future showcase the efforts of those who have truly made their mark on the world.

**Dubai's skyscrapers** poke through the early-morning clouds. The emirate is famous for its super-high structures and is home to the world's tallest building (the Burj Khalifa at 2,717 ft/828 m), and the tallest hotel (the Gevora at 1,168 ft/356 m).

THERE ARE ABOUT 1.47 BILLION CARS IN OPERATION ON THE WORLD'S ROADS.

# ON THE ROAD

Start your **engines**; it's time to take a **trip** down memory **lane** to discover which **inventors** came **first** in the ultimate **road race**.

**No one knew how popular cars would become** when first invented. In 1903, people declared that cars "would never replace the horse" and were "a novelty—a fad." How wrong they were!

**1864**
**First gas-powered car** Austrian inventor Siegfried Marcus added a liquid-fueled engine to a handcart.

**1885**
**First true gas-powered car** Karl Benz built the first car designed to have a gas engine. It looked like a three-wheeled carriage.

**1885**
**First internal combustion-engined bicycle** Although designed only to test the engine, by adding it to a bike Gottlieb Daimler invented the first true motorcycle.

**1886**
**First four-wheeled car with a four-stroke engine** This was built by German engineers Gottlieb Daimler and Wilhelm Maybach.

THE UK-MADE **PEEL P50** IS THE WORLD'S SMALLEST CAR. IT IS 54 IN (137 CM) LONG, 39 IN (99 CM) WIDE, AND WEIGHS 130 LB (59 KG).

THE FASTEST 0–62 MPH (100 K ACCELERATION BY AN ELECTR CAR IS **0.956** SECONDS.

THE TOYOTA COROLLA IS THE WORLD'S BESTSELLING CAR, WITH 50 MILLION SOLD.

### TOPPING 100

A car named *La Jamais Contente* was the first car to top 62 mph (100 km/h), in 1899. Driver Camille Jenatzy achieved 65.79 mph (105.88 km/h) over a distance of 0.6 miles (1 km) in his Belgian-made electric car.

### 1801
**First passenger-carrying car**
On its test run, Richard Trevithick's *Puffing Devil* carried eight people uphill at a speed of 4 mph (6.4 km/h).

### 1769
**First full-scale car**
Frenchman Nicolas-Joseph Cugnot invented a steam-powered tricycle that he called the "steam dray," meaning a cart powered by steam.

### 1894
**First mass-produced motorcycle**
The Hildebrand & Wolfmüller factory in Germany was the first to make motorcycles in large numbers; they produced more than 1,000 in two years.

### 1888
**First true electric car**
The *Flocken Elektrowagen*, invented by Andreas Flocken, is said to be the first practical electric car.

THE **BUGATTI CHIRON** IS THE WORLD'S MOST POWERFUL PRODUCTION CAR. IT HAS A TOP SPEED OF 261 MPH (420 KM/H).

THE MOST EXPENSIVE CAR NUMBER PLATE IS **P-7**. IT SOLD FOR $15 MILLION (£12 MILLION).

THE *FLYING SCOTSMAN* HAS BEEN PAINTED GREEN, BLACK, AND BLUE OVER TIME.

# FULL STEAM AHEAD

**Steam trains** were once a **common sight** on the world's railroads. The locomotives shown here were all the **fastest of their time**.

Stephenson's *Rocket* reached a speed of 30 mph (48 km/h) in 1829.

Many of the *Rocket*'s innovations were so successful that they set the basic layout for locomotives right until the end of the steam era.

THE *FLYING SCOTSMAN* INSPIRED THE HOGWARTS EXPRESS IN THE HARRY POTTER BOOKS.

IN 1830, THE TOM THUMB STEAM LOCOMOTIVE RACED A HORSE AND LOST— BUT ONLY BECAUSE IT BROKE DOWN!

GEORGE STEPHENSON'S *ROCKET* DESIGN WON HIM A COMPETITION PRIZE OF £500.

**On November 30, 1934**, The *Flying Scotsman* became the first locomotive to travel at more than 100 mph (161 km/h).

The *Mallard* reached a top speed of 126 mph (202.6 km/h) on July 3, 1938.

**Stephenson's fabled *Rocket*,** built for the Liverpool and Manchester Railway in 1829, was the template for steam locomotives for the next 150 years. The *Flying Scotsman* and the *Mallard* were perhaps the most iconic steam locomotives of their time.

The *Flying Scotsman* hauled the nonstop **London to Edinburgh** service.

### BIG BOY

Known as "Big Boy," the American Locomotive Company 4000-class steam locomotive had the longest engine body of any locomotive ever built—85.3 ft/25.99 m.

THE **PLAQUE** FIXED TO THE SIDE OF *MALLARD* SHOWS THE WORLD RECORD THAT TO THIS DAY REMAINS UNBROKEN.

BIG BOYS WERE SO LONG THAT ALL **25** OF THEM HAD TO BE SPECIALLY BUILT TO GO AROUND BENDS SAFELY.

APOLLO 11 ASTRONAUTS TOOK THE WRIGHTS' PROPELLER TO THE MOON IN 1969.

# AIR PIONEERS

Imagine being the **first** pilot. Flying **unknown routes** with **untested technology**, these **aviators** must have been **incredibly brave**.

> The first **transatlantic flight** took **16 hours**. The same trip today takes **5 hours**.

### 1970
The first Boeing 747, or jumbo jet, flew between New York and London. The first wide-body plane, it held the record for most passengers (500) until the arrival of the Airbus in 2007.

Wright Flyer

### 1903
The first controlled, powered flight took place in the US with Orville and Wilbur Wright's *Wright Flyer*. It was in the air for only 12 seconds, but the age of flight had begun.

Bell X-1

## FAST FACTS

**It's not just planes** that have set pioneering flight records.

 **1783** First manned, untethered flight: the Montgolfier brothers' hot-air balloon took passengers over Paris, France.

 **1804** First flight by heavier-than-air machine: George Cayley built and flew the first working glider.

 **1907** First manned helicopter flight: the Breguet brothers' Gyroplane No.1 lifted 2 ft (0.6 m) into the air.

**The sky was not the limit** for these intrepid travelers. Each of them has set a record in aviation, whether for being the first aircraft of its type, flying a longer distance, or increasing speed to supersonic.

 **ALTHOUGH WILBUR WON A COIN TOSS FOR THE RIGHT TO BE THE FIRST PERSON TO FLY, ORVILLE FLEW BEFORE HIM.**

 **FRENCH ACTRESS RAYMONDE D LAROCHE WAS THE FIRST-EVER LICENSED FEMALE PILOT, IN 1910.**

THE FIRST BOEING 747 COST $20 MILLION (£16 MILLION) TO BUILD.

Boeing 747

Spirit of St Louis

**1927**
**The first successful solo transatlantic flight** was made by American Charles Lindbergh in the *Spirit of St .Louis*, flying from Long Island, New York, to Paris, France.

Winnie Mae

**1933**
**The first solo flight around the world** was achieved by American Wiley Post in his Lockheed 5C Vega nicknamed *Winnie Mae*, after his daughter. The trip took him 7 days and 18 hours.

**1939**
**The first "turbojet" (jet plane)** was the German Heinkel He 178 V1.

Heinkel He 178

Soviet Tupolev Tu-144

**1975**
**The first supersonic transport** (passenger service to fly faster than the speed of sound, which is 767 mph, or 1,235 km/h) was the Soviet Tupolev Tu-144.

**2004**
**The fastest aircraft with an air-breathing (jet) engine** is the unmanned NASA X-43A. It reached 6,755 mph (10,871.12 km/h) on November 16.

NASA X-43

**1947**
**The first person to break the sound barrier** in an aircraft was US pilot Chuck Yeager in the Bell X-1. Aircraft speed is measured in Mach: Mach 1 is the speed of sound, Mach 2 is twice as fast, and so on.

# 1932

IN **1932**, AMELIA EARHART BECAME THE FIRST WOMAN TO FLY SOLO ACROSS THE ATLANTIC.

GLADYS ROY, AMERICAN DAREDEVIL AND STUNT PILOT OF THE 1920S, DANCED A **CHARLESTON** AND PLAYED TENNIS ON AN AIRCRAFT WING IN FLIGHT!

WOODEN HYDROPLANE *SPIRIT OF AUSTRALIA* WAS BUILT BY ITS PILOT.

# THE NEED
# FOR SPEED

The world's official **land-speed record** is a staggering **763.035 mph** (1,227.985 km/h). It was set by British RAF fighter pilot **Andy Green** on October 15, 1997, in a vehicle called **Thrust SSC**.

The **SSC** was the **first car** to almost break the **sound barrier**.

### FUTURE CHALLENGER

Plans are under way to attempt to break the land-speed record. The British-designed Bloodhound is planned to travel at more than 1,000 mph (1,609 km/h).

**Two Rolls-Royce Spey 205** turbofan engines powered the vehicle. These engines are normally found on F-4 Phantom II jet fighters.

ANDY GREEN, A FORMER **RAF FIGHTER** PILOT, WAS CHOSEN FROM AROUND 30 CANDIDATES TO DRIVE THRUST SSC.

THE SONIC BOOM PRODUCED BY THIS VEHICLE WAS SO LOUD THAT IT SET OFF **CAR ALARMS** IN A TOWN 10 MILES (16 KM) AWAY.

SPIRIT OF AUSTRALIA IS NOW AT SYDNEY'S NATIONAL MARITIME MUSEUM.

## FAST FACTS

**There are several** speed-based records up for grabs.

**Water-speed record** by Ken Warby in *Spirit of Australia*, 1977
317.58 mph (511.09 km/h)

**Motorcycle record** by Rocky Robinson in *Top Oil-Ack Attack*, 2010
376.363 mph (605.697 km/h)

**Land-speed record** by Andy Green in *Thrust SSC*, 1997
763.035 mph (1,227.985 km/h)

**Although the car** was designed and built in Britain, the world-record attempt took place in the Black Rock Desert, Nevada. The desert's flat, lakebed surface made it the perfect site for land-speed record attempts. To set the record, Andy Green had to drive Thrust twice within an hour, in opposite directions over a measured distance of 1 mile (1.6 km).

**The engines burned** 4.75 gallons (18 liters) of fuel per second.

**763.035 mph (1,227.985 km/h)**

**Including the streamlined tail fin**, the car's total length was 54 ft (16.5 m). It was 12 ft (3.7 m) wide and weighed 12 tons.

**TO ENSURE AN EVEN TRACK, THRUST SSC'S TEAM REMOVED ROCKY DEBRIS BY HAND**—A PROCESS CALLED "FODDING."

**TODAY, THRUST SSC IS ON DISPLAY AT THE TRANSPORT MUSEUM IN COVENTRY (UK).**

THE QINGHAI–TIBET RAILWAY COST $4.2 BILLION (£3.4 BILLION) TO BUILD …

# ON THE RIGHT TRACK

**TRAILBLAZING TRAINS**

**The fastest train on a national railroad system:**
A TGV V150 (above) reached a world-record speed of 357.16 mph (574.8 km/h) on the high-speed line between Paris and Strasbourg in France on April 3, 2007.

**The fastest train:**
On January 16, 2014, the Chinese-made experimental high-speed train, the CIT500, set a world record of 376 mph (605 km/h).

**The longest train route:**
The world's longest train route runs 6,380 miles (10,267 km) between Moscow (Russia) and Pyongyang (North Korea). It takes 206 hours to complete the journey.

**The route**, one of the world's most picturesque, passes towering peaks, shimmering lakes, and gigantic glaciers.

**The train cars** are pressurized, like the cabin on a plane. Oxygen levels are increased as the train reaches higher altitudes.

 AS TRACK WAS LAID, **OXYGEN-SUPPLY** AND MEDICAL STOPS WERE ALSO BUILT TO HELP WORKERS WITH ALTITUDE SICKNESS.

 AT TANGGULA, THE WORLD'S HIGHEST RAILROAD STATION, OXYGEN LEVELS ARE **60** PERCENT OF THOSE AT SEA LEVEL.

... AND INCLUDES THE WORLD'S HIGHEST SECTION OF TRACK: 16,640 FT (5,072 M).

**Technology** has **transformed** the way people travel. **Trains** today enable us to go **higher, faster, and farther** than ever before.

**The Qinghai–Tibet railway** is 1,215 miles (1,956 km) long and connects the cities of Xining (China) with Lhasa (Tibet).

The **journey from Xining to Lhasa takes 20 hours 55 minutes to** complete.

**The trains were specially designed** to work at the extreme altitude. Around 597 miles (960 km) of the track sit above 13,123 ft (4,000 m).

**TRAIN WINDOWS ARE COATED TO PROTECT PEOPLE FROM POWERFUL HIGH-ALTITUDE SOLAR RAYS.**

IN SUMMER 2023, THE **QINGHAI–TIBET RAILWAY** CARRIED MORE THAN 4.35 MILLION PASSENGERS.

THE AIRBUS A380'S WINGSPAN IS WIDER THAN 32 DOUBLE-DECKER BUSES.

# AWESOME AIRCRAFT

*Largest airship:*
Hindenburg LZ 129
**804 ft (245 m)**

**Creating bigger and better aircraft** has been a challenge since the first powered flight in 1903. But size isn't always an indication of superiority: the Hindenburg (which carried a maximum of 72 passengers) lasted just 14 months before being destroyed by fire in 1937.

*Largest cargo aircraft:*
Antonov An-225
**276 ft (84 m) long**

*Largest commercial passenger aircraft:*
Airbus A380
**240 ft (73 m) long**

*Largest flying boat:*
Hughes H-4 Hercules
**219 ft (67 m) long**

WHEN **BUMBLE BEE II's** ENGINE FAILED, IT WAS DESTROYED AND ITS PILOT SERIOUSLY INJURED.

THE **MIL MI-26** HELICOPTER MADE HISTORY AS THE FIRST TO TAKE OFF WITH AN EIGHT-BLADE MAIN ROTOR.

THE AIRBUS A380 CONTAINS MORE THAN 300 MILES (480 KM) OF ELECTRICAL CABLES.

From **huge wingspans** to the ability to carry **great weights** or just being the **largest** of their type, here are some of the **biggest** aircraft to have flown.

Largest glider:
Messerschmitt ME 321
**92 ft (28 m) long**

The Hindenburg airship was the largest object ever to have flown.

Largest helicopter:
Mil Mi-26
**131 ft (40 m) long**

Largest biplane:
Navy Curtiss NC-4
**68 ft (20.8 m) long**

**FAST FACTS**

**The smallest plane** that could carry a person was the Bumble Bee II, a biplane that made one flight in 1988 before crashing. It was smaller than an Airbus A380 engine and had a wingspan just 5 ft 6 in (1.68 m) wide.

A380 engine fan:
9.7 ft (2.95 m) wide

Bumble Bee II:
8.8 ft (2.69 m) long

ONLY ONE HUGHES H-4 HERCULES FLYING BOAT WAS BUILT. IT FLEW JUST ONCE, PILOTED BY ITS BUILDER, US BILLIONAIRE HOWARD HUGHES.

HINDENBURG WAS FILLED WITH FLAMMABLE HYDROGEN, WHICH CAUSED THE FATAL 1937 FIRE.

### GIANT OF THE SKY

**At 804 ft (245 m) in length**, the *Hindenburg* was the largest rigid airship ever built and still holds the record as the largest aircraft ever to fly. It was built in Germany and flew from March 1936 until it was destroyed by fire on May 6, 1937, while attempting to land at Lakehurst, New Jersey.

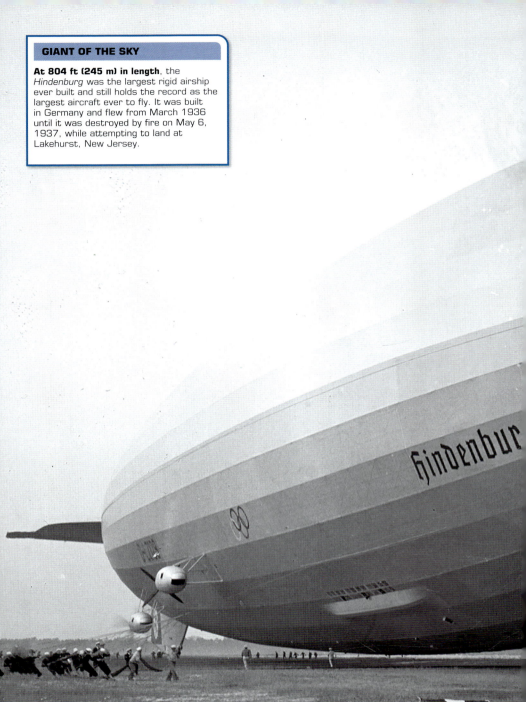

THE COLLIDER TOOK 10 YEARS TO BUILD AND COST $4.75 BILLION (£3.8 BILLION).

**Magnets inside the LHC have to be kept at −456°F (−271°C)—that's colder than outer space.**

**Inside the beam pipe,** particles travel at high speed in different directions and smash into each other.

 AROUND **10,000** PEOPLE, INCLUDING SCIENTISTS, ENGINEERS, AND STUDENTS, FROM 60 COUNTRIES HELPED CREATE THE LHC.

 THE COLLIDER'S NAME COMES FROM THE HADRONS, OR POSITIVELY CHARGED **PROTONS**, FORMED INSIDE IT.

UNFORTUNATELY, THE LARGE HADRON COLLIDER IS NOT OPEN TO VISITORS.

# COLOSSAL COLLIDER

Deep underground in France and Switzerland lies the **Large Hadron Collider (LHC)**—the world's **largest machine** and **most powerful** particle accelerator. Scientists are using it to find out more about **particle physics**.

**The Large Hadron Collider** is conducting an experiment on a huge scale. It is smashing together two beams of particles at super-high speed around its vast 17-mile (27 km) long ring. Scientists are trying to reproduce what happened during the Big Bang.

### UNDERGROUND EXPERIMENTS

**The particle accelerator** is made up of two huge underground rings. The smaller one, the Super Proton Synchrotron, shown in blue on the right, accelerates atoms to almost the speed of light before "injecting" them into the Large Hadron Collider (shown in yellow), where they smash together at four measuring stations spaced out around the ring.

SOME SCIENTISTS BASED AT THE LHC HAVE WON THE **NOBEL PRIZE** IN PHYSICS FOR THEIR PIONEERING WORK.

THERE ARE PLANS TO BUILD A CIRCULAR COLLIDER MEASURING **57** MILES (91 KM), ALMOST FOUR TIMES LONGER THAN THIS ONE!

IN 1995 BAGGER 293 COST $100 MILLION (£80 MILLION) TO BUILD.

# MEGA MACHINES

Some machines are **mind-bogglingly big**. They can be used to **shift earth**, to **carry enormous objects** (such as space rockets), or to help **dig open-cast mines**.

**Giant buckets** on this huge wheel carve through the earth.

**At 315 ft (96 m) tall**, Bagger 293 is also the world's highest terrestrial vehicle.

### LARGEST SELF-POWERED VEHICLE

Weighing 3,325 tons (3,016 metric tons) and measuring 131 x 114 ft (40 x 35 m), NASA's Crawler Transporter 2 (used to carry spacecraft) is the world's largest self-powered vehicle.

**BAGGER 293 TOOK THREE WEEKS TO TRAVEL 80 MILES (130 KM) FROM THE FACTORY TO THE MINE WHERE IT IS LOCATED.**

**THIS MACHINE DOES THE SAME AMOUNT OF WORK AS 40,000 MINERS 24 HOURS A DAY, SEVEN DAYS A WEEK.**

## SUPER-SIZE BAGGER 293 IS OPERATED BY A CREW OF FIVE PEOPLE.

**Weighing a colossal 15,650 tons (14,200 metric tons)**, the Bagger 293 Bucket Excavator is the world's heaviest land vehicle. It belongs to a German mining company and is used to excavate an enormous mine near Hambach, western Germany.

Bagger 293 removes enough material to fill **2,500 railroad wagons** every day.

**ITS WHEEL IS 71 FT (22 M) WIDE AND ITS 18 BUCKETS ROTATE TO SCOOP UP EARTH AND COAL.**

**IT CAN DIG OUT HUGE AMOUNTS OF COAL WORTH $1 BILLION (£800 MILLION) A YEAR.**

THE GREAT WALL OF CHINA TOOK MORE THAN 2,000 YEARS TO COMPLETE.

# WONDER WALLS

Walls have been built for **thousands of years** to give **privacy, defense, protection**, and even **segregation**. Those that have stood the **test of time** still make history today.

In 1985, three Chinese friends became the first to **walk the wall**; it took them **508 days**.

**Longest Roman wall**
Hadrian's Wall extends for 73 miles (117 km) across the north of England. It holds records for being the world's longest Roman wall and the longest wall in Europe. The Roman emperor Hadrian ordered that it be built in 122 CE to provide protection from the Barbarians in the north.

**World's longest wall**
The Great Wall of China, stretching a whopping 5,500 miles (8,851 km) across the north of China, is the world's longest wall. It was first built to protect China against invaders from the north. Some sections of the wall are 39 ft (12 m) tall and 32 ft (10 m) thick.

 HADRIAN'S WALL WAS BUILT BY ABOUT 15,000 **CITIZEN-SOLDIERS** FROM THE ROMAN ARMY AND WAS SIX YEARS IN THE MAKING.

 ONLY ABOUT **10** PERCENT OF HADRIAN'S WALL IS VISIBLE TODAY— THE REST WAS DESTROYED, ERODED, OR BURIED.

THE MARKS MADE BY ANCIENT BUILDERS CAN STILL BE SEEN ON THE GREAT WALL.

### Oldest temple walls
The most ancient temple walls found so far support the glorious temple of Gobekli Tepe in Sanliurfa, Türkiye. These great carved stones were carefully positioned by ancient builders about 11,500 years ago.

### Oldest city walls
The first city walls were built around the ancient city of Jericho, Israel. Built from about 8000 BCE, these strong stone walls stand 13 ft (4 m) high.

### Longest walls around a fort
These are found at the Kumbhalgarh Fort in Rajasthan, India. Built in the 15th century, the walls measure 22 miles (36 km) long and 16 ft (5 m) wide. Legends claim that eight horses could run side by side along the top of the walls!

Walls have been built for centuries around castles and cities or along national borders to keep people in or out. The world's oldest walls have become historic and iconic landmarks.

### FAST FACTS

**The Great Wall of China** is one of the most popular places in the world to visit. Here are a few more tourist attractions and the number of visitors per year.

| Grand Bazaar, Türkiye | Las Vegas Strip, US | Great Wall of China, China | Eiffel Tower, France |
|---|---|---|---|
| 40 million visitors | 39 million visitors | 9 million visitors | 7 million visitors |

THE WALLS OF JERICHO WERE FIRST BUILT AROUND 8000 BCE AND REBUILT MANY TIMES SINCE THEN.

THE INTRICATE ANIMAL IMAGES AND SYMBOLS ON THE WALLS OF GOBEKLI TEPE WERE CARVED BY ANCIENT HUNTER-GATHERERS.

THE TOP OF THE BURJ KHALIFA IS VISIBLE 60 MILES (95 KM) AWAY.

# RECORD-BREAKING HEIGHTS

Throughout history, a total of **25 structures** have held the accolade of being the **world's tallest building**. The title currently belongs to the 2,717 ft (828 m) **Burj Khalifa** in Dubai, UAE.

## FAST FACTS

**The Jeddah Tower** in Saudi Arabia is set to become the world's tallest building once it is finally completed (construction began in 2013 but has been delayed). At a staggering 3,281 ft (1,000 m) tall, it will be 564 ft (172 m) taller than Dubai's Burj Khalifa.

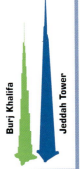

## THE GREATEST OF THE PYRAMIDS

The Great Pyramid of Giza, situated near Cairo, Egypt, was built over a period of 20 years, ending around 2560 BCE. At 481 ft (146.6 m), it was the tallest man-made structure in the world for a record-breaking 3,800 years.

**Great Pyramid of Giza, near Cairo, Egypt**
481 ft (146.6 m)
2560 BCE–1240 CE

**Old St. Paul's Cathedral, London, UK**
493 ft (150.2 m)
1240–1311

**Lincoln Cathedral, Lincoln, UK**
525 ft (160 m)
1311–1548

**St. Mary's Church, Stralsund, Germany**
495 ft (151 m)
1548–1647

**Strasbourg Cathedral, Strasbourg, France**
466 ft (142 m)
1647–1874

**Woolworth Building, New York, NY, US**
792 ft (241.4 m)
1913–1930

**Chrysler Building, New York, NY, US**
1,046 ft (318.8 m)
1929–1931

THE BURJ KHALIFA HAS THE MOST STORIES (**163**) AND THE HIGHEST PUBLIC OBSERVATION DECK, ON THE 124TH FLOOR.

THE WEIGHT OF ALL THE CONCRETE IN THE BURJ KHALIFA IS ABOUT THE SAME AS 100,000 **ELEPHANTS**.

**AT LEAST 12,000 BUILDERS WERE INVOLVED IN THE BURJ KHALIFA'S CONSTRUCTION.**

The earliest of the world's tallest buildings were pyramids and religious structures. However, the increased use of steel in construction from the late 19th century eventually led to the birth of the skyscraper.

> It is **10°F (6°C)** cooler at the **top** of the Burj Khalifa than it is at the **bottom**.

**Taipei 101,** Taipei, Taiwan
1,671 ft (509.2 m)
**2004–2010**

**Willis Tower (formerly Sears Tower),** Chicago, IL, US
1,450 ft (442 m)
**1974–1998**

**Empire State Building,** New York, NY, US
1,250 ft (381 m)
**1931–1972**

**World Trade Center,** New York, NY, US
1,368 ft (417 m)
**1972–1974**

**Petronas Towers,** Kuala Lumpur, Malaysia
1,483 ft (451.9 m)
**1998–2004**

**Burj Khalifa,** Dubai, UAE
2,717 ft (828 m)
**2010–**

**Jeddah Tower,** Jeddah, Saudi Arabia
3,281 ft (1,000 m)

 AT **32** FT (10 M) PER SECOND, THE BURJ KHALIFA'S ELEVATOR REACHES ITS OBSERVATION DECK WITHIN A MINUTE.

 BURJ KHALIFA'S SPIRE IS DESIGNED TO RESEMBLE THE **HYMENOCALLIS SPIDER LILY,** A DESERT FLOWER.

# Engineering data

## MEGA BUILDINGS

Big buildings aren't always **high**; some simply **cover an enormous area**. Here are two of the **world's biggest buildings by area**.

**LARGEST FLOOR AREA**
OPENED IN 2013, **THE NEW CENTURY GLOBAL CENTER IS A MULTIPURPOSE BUILDING IN CHENGDU, CHINA**. IT HAS THE LARGEST FLOOR AREA OF ANY BUILDING IN THE WORLD— **18.3 MILLION SQ FT (1.7 MILLION SQ M)**. IT'S SO BIG, IT COULD FIT **NEARLY FOUR VATICAN CITIES** INSIDE.

**WORLD'S LARGEST MUSEUM**
ORIGINALLY BUILT AS A FORTRESS, **THE LOUVRE, IN PARIS, FRANCE, IS THE WORLD'S LARGEST MUSEUM**. IT COVERS AN AREA OF **2.26 MILLION SQ FT (210,000 SQ M)**.

## TERRIFIC TUNNELS

**TUNNELS** are used to **TRANSPORT TRAINS, CARS**, and even **WATER**. Some pass **under mountains**, and others even go **under the sea**, but which are **THE WORLD'S LONGEST?**

**LONGEST ROAD TUNNEL:**
LAERDAL TUNNEL (LAERDAL, AURLAND, NORWAY)—15.2 MILES (24.51 KM)

**LONGEST UNDERSEA TUNNEL:**
CHANNEL TUNNEL (ENGLAND–FRANCE)—23.5 MILES (37.9 KM)

**WORLD'S LONGEST TUNNEL WITH UNDERSEA SECTION:**
SEIKAN TUNNEL (JAPAN)—33.46 MILES (53.85 KM), OF WHICH 14.5 MILES (23.3 KM) LIES UNDER THE SEABED.

**LONGEST WATER SUPPLY TUNNEL:**
DELAWARE AQUEDUCT (NEW YORK, US)—85.1 MILES (137 KM)

**Carved** through the **Swiss Alps**, the **Gotthard Base Tunnel**, opened on June 1, 2016, is the **longest railroad tunnel** in the world.

Chrüzlistock
8,914 FT (2,717 M)

← NORTH (to Zurich, Switzerland)

SWITZERLAND

**LONGEST RAILROAD TUNNEL:** GOTTHARD BASE TUNNEL (SWITZERLAND)—35.5 MILES (57.1 KM)

**THE LONGEST CONTINUOUS BRIDGE OVER WATER, AT 24 MILES (38 KM), IS IN LOUISIANA.**

**SITTING 1,854 FT (565M) OVER CHINA'S BEIPAN RIVER, DUGE BRIDGE IS THE WORLD'S HIGHEST.**

MOROCCO'S SEAWATER ORTHLIEB POOL IS THE WORLD'S LARGEST SWIMMING POOL.

## WORK IN PROGRESS

**Some buildings don't get finished:** some start with huge ambitions before **being abandoned;** others are **still not completed** more than **one hundred years** after **work started on them**.

**WORK ON THE SAGRADA FAMÍLIA,** AN ORNATE CATHEDRAL DESIGNED BY THE FAMOUS ARTIST GAUDÍ IN BARCELONA, SPAIN, WAS STARTED IN 1882. IT STILL HAS NOT BEEN FINISHED TO THIS DAY.

**THE NAKHEEL TOWER IN DUBAI, UAE,** WAS DESIGNED TO BE THE TALLEST TOWER IN THE WORLD, AT MORE THAN 3,280 FT (1 KM) TO THE SPIRE. WORK STARTED IN 2008, BUT WAS CANCELED IN 2009 HAVING RACKED UP COSTS OF MORE THAN $38 BILLION (£27.3 BILLION).

# BRILLIANT BUILDINGS

**Not all buildings** are made of **concrete** or **bricks**. Here are some **unusual big builds** from **around the world**.

### TALLEST WOODEN PAGODA
BUILT BACK IN 1056, THE SAKYAMUNI PAGODA IN SHANXI, CHINA, STANDS 220.8 FT (67.31 M) TALL. IT HAS ENDURED MORE THAN 960 YEARS OF HARSH WEATHER AND EVEN EARTHQUAKES.

### BIGGEST PAPER BUILDING
THAI PAPER HOUSE WAS CONSTRUCTED IN BANGKOK, THAILAND, IN OCTOBER 2003. MADE ENTIRELY OF PAPER, IT MEASURED 49.8 FT (15.2 M) WIDE, 58.7 FT (17.9 M) LONG, AND STOOD 21 FT (6.4 M) TALL.

### BIGGEST MUD BUILDING
AT 328 FT (100 M) LONG, 131 FT (40 M) WIDE, AND 52 FT (16 M) TALL, THE GRAND MOSQUE OF DJENNE IN MALI IS THE WORLD'S LARGEST BUILDING MADE OF ADOBE (MUD). BASED ON AN 11TH-CENTURY DESIGN, IT WAS BUILT IN 1907.

**iz Vatgira** ,783 FT (2,982 M)

**Pizzo dell'Uomo** 8,737 FT (2,663 M)

**The tunnel is named for** the Saint-Gotthard Massif, under which it runs.

**SOUTH (to Milan, Italy)** ➡

**SAINT-GOTTHARD MASSIF**

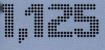

**FRANCE'S MILLAU VIADUCT IS THE WORLD'S TALLEST BRIDGE, MEASURING 1,125 FT (343 M) FROM TOP TO BOTTOM.**

**CROSSED SINCE 850 BCE, TURKEY'S CARAVAN BRIDGE IS THE WORLD'S OLDEST USABLE BRIDGE.**

# Living world

The natural world offers a rich and colorful tapestry of amazing animals and plants. The age of the dinosaurs saw giant contenders for size and strength. Today, a huge variety of species live alongside each other, unknowingly winning titles for the most fabulous flora and fauna on Earth.

**Millions of monarch butterflies** make the longest butterfly migration, flying 3,000 miles (4,830 km) from Canada and North America to California and Mexico to spend the winter. Only butterflies born in late summer and early fall undertake this incredible round trip and they make it only once in their lifetime.

THE HUMMINGBIRD IS THE ONLY BIRD THAT CAN FLY BACKWARD.

# ANIMAL RECORDS

Which animal has the **longest nose**, the biggest eye, or the **best eyesight?** You might be **surprised** by the answers.

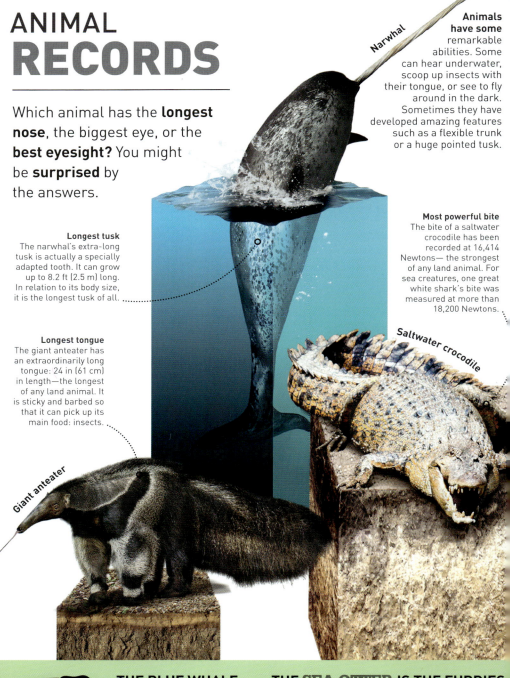

**Narwhal**

**Animals have some** remarkable abilities. Some can hear underwater, scoop up insects with their tongue, or see to fly around in the dark. Sometimes they have developed amazing features such as a flexible trunk or a huge pointed tusk.

**Longest tusk**
The narwhal's extra-long tusk is actually a specially adapted tooth. It can grow up to 8.2 ft (2.5 m) long. In relation to its body size, it is the longest tusk of all.

**Most powerful bite**
The bite of a saltwater crocodile has been recorded at 16,414 Newtons— the strongest of any land animal. For sea creatures, one great white shark's bite was measured at more than 18,200 Newtons.

**Saltwater crocodile**

**Longest tongue**
The giant anteater has an extraordinarily long tongue: 24 in (61 cm) in length—the longest of any land animal. It is sticky and barbed so that it can pick up its main food: insects.

**Giant anteater**

THE BLUE WHALE AND **AFRICAN ELEPHANT** ARE, RESPECTIVELY, THE BIGGEST SEA AND LAND CREATURES.

THE **SEA OTTER** IS THE FURRIES CREATURE, WITH UP TO 160,000 HAIRS PER SQUARE CENTIMETER.

A CUVIER'S BEAKED WHALE HELD ITS BREATH FOR 3 HOURS AND 42 MINUTES.

**Widest hearing range**
A porpoise has a wide hearing range of up to 150 kHz (kilohertz), a dog up to 46 kHz, and a human up to 20 kHz. The American Shad fish's range (up to 180 kHz) helps it avoid the predatory porpoise.

Porpoise

**Longest nose**
The African elephant's trunk is the longest nose in the animal kingdom. As well as being sensitive enough to pick up small items and strong enough to bat away a lion, it can detect a huge range of scents.

Elephant trunk

**Best insect night vision**
This bee—the nocturnal carpenter bee—can fly at night and still find food and pick out colors even when there is no moon. Nocturnal hawk moths can also see colors at night.

Carpenter bees

The African elephant also has the largest ears—over 3.3 ft (1 m) long.

**Biggest eye**
Colossal squid are huge creatures so it's not surprising that their eyes are the largest in the animal kingdom. Each eye measures about 11 in (28 cm) in diameter—about the same as a dinner plate.

Colossal squid

THE TOCO TOUCAN'S EYE-CATCHING ORANGE BEAK MEASURES 8 IN (19 CM) LONG AND TAKES UP ONE-THIRD OF ITS BODY SIZE.

A SNOW LEOPARD LEAPT 38 FT (11.7 M)—STRAIGHT INTO THE RECORD BOOKS AS THE LONGEST JUMP BY A CAT.

**104** AUSTRALIAN TIGER BEETLES CAN RUN AT 8.2 FT (2.5 M) PER SECOND ...

# LIFE IN THE
# FAST LANE

Meet the **speediest** creatures on **land**, in **water**, and in the **air**. In a head-to-head (or wing-to-tail) **race**, which one runs away with **gold**?

Elephant
15 mph (24.5 km/h)

27.8 mph (44.7 km/h)
Athlete

Dolphin
18.6 mph (30 km/h)

*If people ran as fast as cheetahs, the 100 m record would be 3.6 seconds.*

THE **PEREGRINE FALCON** IS THE WORLD'S FASTEST CREATURE, BUT ITS TYPICAL SPEED IS ABOUT 56 MPH (90 KM/H).

15

ELEPHANTS ARE SO BIG THEY CAN'T RUN FOR LONG, BUT THEY USUALLY WALK MORE THAN **15 MILES** (25 KM) A DAY.

... IF THEY WERE HUMAN-SIZE, THAT'S AS FAST AS 497 MPH (800 KM/H).

**The cheetah is well known** for being the fastest sprinter on land, but it is just out-paced by the ocean-going sailfish. Both are left trailing far behind the quickest airborne animal: the peregrine falcon. When this bird dives for prey, it reaches speeds almost four times faster than the cheetah.

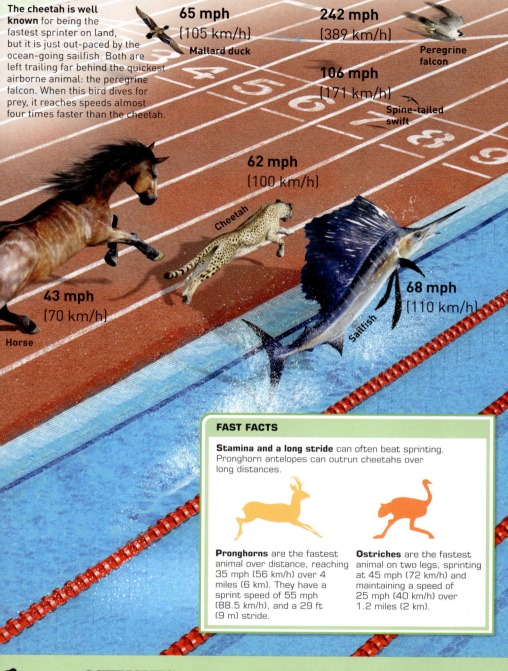

**65 mph (105 km/h)** Mallard duck
**242 mph (389 km/h)** Peregrine falcon
**106 mph (171 km/h)** Spine-tailed swift
**62 mph (100 km/h)** Cheetah
**43 mph (70 km/h)** Horse
**68 mph (110 km/h)** Sailfish

## FAST FACTS

**Stamina and a long stride** can often beat sprinting. Pronghorn antelopes can outrun cheetahs over long distances.

**Pronghorns** are the fastest animal over distance, reaching 35 mph (56 km/h) over 4 miles (6 km). They have a sprint speed of 55 mph (88.5 km/h), and a 29 ft (9 m) stride.

**Ostriches** are the fastest animal on two legs, sprinting at 45 mph (72 km/h) and maintaining a speed of 25 mph (40 km/h) over 1.2 miles (2 km).

**OSTRICHES** ARE TOO HEAVY TO FLY. THEY RUN AT HIGH SPEED ON TWO LONG, STRONG LEGS TO ESCAPE PREDATORS.

THE BLACK MARLIN IS NEARLY AS FAST AS THE SAILFISH, BUT ITS USUAL SWIMMING SPEED IS ABOUT **25** MPH (40 KM/H).

A GROUP OF FLAMINGOS IS CALLED A FLAMBOYANCE.

### FAST FACTS

**The largest bird**, the ostrich, also lays the largest egg. One example weighed 91.35 oz (2.59 kg). The smallest egg is laid by a vervain hummingbird and it weighs a little more than 0.01 oz (0.36 g). A medium-size chicken's egg, by comparison, weighs 1.87 oz (53 g).

Hummingbird egg

Chicken egg

Ostrich egg

**Most talkative**
The African gray parrot is a great talker; it can learn as many as 1,000 words.

**Smallest bird**
The tiny bee hummingbird is the smallest bird. It is just 2 in (5–6 cm) long.

**Largest bird**
The ostrich can grow up to 9 ft (2.8 m) tall—making it the biggest bird of all. It's also the fastest bird on land—capable of running at speeds of 45 mph (72 km/h).

**HUMMINGBIRDS** HAVE A VERY FAST METABOLISM AND EAT UP TO 12 TIMES THEIR BODY WEIGHT IN SWEET NECTAR EVERY DAY FOR ENERGY.

**AFRICAN GRAY PARROTS** CAN RECOGNIZE AT LEAST 80 DIFFERENT THINGS AND REACT TO COLORS AND SHAPES!

AN ALBATROSS CAN FLY 600 MILES (965 KM) WITHOUT FLAPPING ITS WINGS.

# BRILLIANT BIRDS

Birds can **soar in the skies** and **race** along the ground. Some have **huge beaks** for catching fish, while others are so tiny they collect **nectar** from flowers.

**Longest beak**
The bird with the longest beak is the Australian pelican. Its bill can be up to 18 in (47 cm) long—that's as long as three hot dogs!

**Longest wingspan**
These enormous wings belong to a wandering albatross. The wings stretch for 8.2–11.5 ft (2.5–3.5 m) and help the albatross glide effortlessly along on currents of air.

**Oldest bird**
Is this the oldest bird ever? It's certainly the oldest flamingo. Named "Greater," this flamingo lived in Adelaide Zoo, Australia, until it was 83 years old.

A wandering albatross was recorded flying 3,728 miles (6,000 km) in 12 days.

 THE AUSTRALIAN PELICAN'S GIANT BEAK ACTS LIKE A FISHING NET. IT HOLDS UP TO **3 GALLONS (13 LITERS)** OF SEAWATER.

 THE FLAMINGO'S DISTINCTIVE BRIGHT PINK FEATHERS COME FROM PIGMENTS INSIDE THE SHRIMP IT LOVES TO EAT.

**BIRDS OF A FEATHER**

**This spectacular display** of bright green budgerigars takes place over the grassland of central Australia. Up to 10,000 birds swoop down each morning looking for water, forming the largest collection of budgerigars in the world. They pause for a few seconds to drink before taking off again.

**TWO MILLION AFRICAN WILDEBEEST MIGRATE 300 MILES (480 KM) EACH YEAR.**

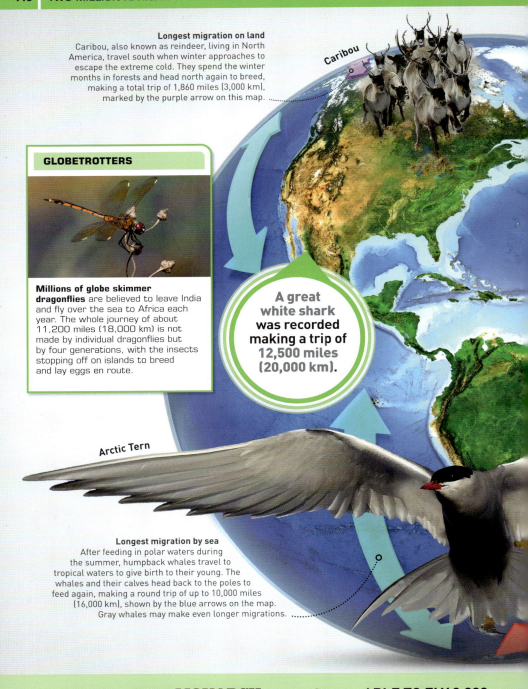

**Longest migration on land**
Caribou, also known as reindeer, living in North America, travel south when winter approaches to escape the extreme cold. They spend the winter months in forests and head north again to breed, making a total trip of 1,860 miles (3,000 km), marked by the purple arrow on this map.

Caribou

### GLOBETROTTERS

**Millions of globe skimmer dragonflies** are believed to leave India and fly over the sea to Africa each year. The whole journey of about 11,200 miles (18,000 km) is not made by individual dragonflies but by four generations, with the insects stopping off on islands to breed and lay eggs en route.

**A great white shark was recorded making a trip of 12,500 miles (20,000 km).**

Arctic Tern

**Longest migration by sea**
After feeding in polar waters during the summer, humpback whales travel to tropical waters to give birth to their young. The whales and their calves head back to the poles to feed again, making a round trip of up to 10,000 miles (16,000 km), shown by the blue arrows on the map. Gray whales may make even longer migrations.

**ADULT MONARCH BUTTERFLIES BORN IN SUMMER LIVE FOR ONLY FOUR TO FIVE WEEKS. THOSE BORN LATER CAN LIVE UP TO NINE MONTHS.**

**ABLE TO FLY 9,300 MILES (15,000 KM) IN ONE TRIP, THE WANDERING ALBATROSS IS WELL NAMED.**

A MALE TIGER CAN ROAM AN AREA OF UP TO 770 SQUARE MILES (2,000 SQ KM).

Humpback whale

### FAST FACTS

**Atlantic salmon** have a remarkable life cycle. Each fish migrates from the river where it was born out to sea. Once they are adults, they make their way back to the same river where they were born to breed and lay their eggs. Then they return to the ocean.

Spawning → Eggs → Immature fish → Young fish → Adult

**Many animals, especially birds,** migrate away from the winter cold. They often set off in groups and follow the same route every year, the young learning the way from their parents.

**Longest migration by air**
The Arctic tern is a remarkable bird; it makes the longest migration of any animal. Each year it spends summer in the Arctic, then flies to the Antarctic for the summer, before returning to the Arctic again—a round trip of 46,600 miles (75,000 km)—shown by the red arrow on the map.

# A LONG WAY TO GO

Every year, **huge numbers** of animals set off on **long trips** in search of food, a mate, or warmer climes. As well as being long, these **migrations** are also **hazardous**.

 **EVERY YEAR IN THE ANTARCTIC, EMPEROR PENGUINS WALK FOR 75 MILES (120 KM) IN FREEZING WEATHER TO THEIR BREEDING SITES.**

 **THE BAR-TAILED GODWIT MAKES AN EPIC SUMMERTIME FLIGHT FROM ALASKA TO NEW ZEALAND.**

DEVIL RAYS GOT THEIR NAME BECAUSE OF THEIR TWO FRONT-FACING HORNS.

# GIANTS OF THE DEEP

The **blue whale** is well known as the **world's biggest** animal, but how do other large **sea creatures** measure up?

> Lion's mane jellyfish tentacles are longer than a blue whale.

Largest jellyfish: Lion's mane jellyfish 7.5 ft (2.3 m) wide

The jellyfish's bell (body) may be large, but it's no comparison to its longest tentacles, which can stretch for 120 ft (36.5 m).

World's largest-ever animal: Blue whale 107 ft (32.6 m)

The water in the oceans supports the weight of marine animals' bodies, which helps them grow to sizes that wouldn't be possible on land. An average blue whale weighs 30 times more than an elephant—no legs could stand up to that!

THE GIANT **LION'S MANE JELLYFISH** HAS A HIGHLY TOXIC STING, BUT TURTLES ARE IMMUNE AND STILL PREY ON IT.

**ORCAS** EAT UP TO 500 LB (227 KG) OF FOOD A DAY. THEY HUNT TOGETHER IN PODS AND ARE ALSO CALLED "KILLER WHALES."

THE BLUE WHALE HAS A HEART THE SIZE OF A CAR. | 113

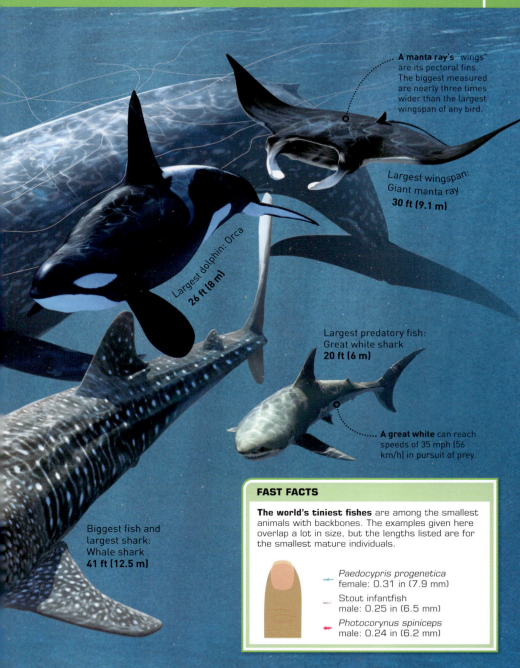

**A manta ray's "wings"** are its pectoral fins. The biggest measured are nearly three times wider than the largest wingspan of any bird.

Largest wingspan: Giant manta ray
**30 ft (9.1 m)**

Largest dolphin: Orca
**26 ft (8 m)**

Largest predatory fish: Great white shark
**20 ft (6 m)**

**A great white** can reach speeds of 35 mph (56 km/h) in pursuit of prey.

Biggest fish and largest shark: Whale shark
**41 ft (12.5 m)**

### FAST FACTS

**The world's tiniest fishes** are among the smallest animals with backbones. The examples given here overlap a lot in size, but the lengths listed are for the smallest mature individuals.

*Paedocypris progenetica* female: 0.31 in (7.9 mm)
*Stout infantfish* male: 0.25 in (6.5 mm)
*Photocorynus spiniceps* male: 0.24 in (6.2 mm)

 A **GREAT WHITE SHARK'S** 300 TEETH ARE CONTINUALLY REPLACED—IT GROWS THOUSANDS OVER ITS LIFETIME!

 SHARKS HAVE AN AMAZING SENSE OF SMELL. THEY CAN DETECT A DROP OF BLOOD IN **1** MILLION DROPS OF WATER.

*UMILIPES PERSEPHONE IS A MILLIPEDE WITH A RECORD-BREAKING 1,306 LEGS.*

# MINI BEASTS

These **mighty mini beasts** might not be welcome at your next picnic. They are some of the **heavyweights and giants** of the insect world.

**Fastest flier**
When a horsefly is in pursuit of a mate, it has been known to reach speeds of 90 mph (145 km/h).

**Largest caterpillar**
At 6 in (15 cm) in length, the hickory horned devil caterpillar is almost as long as a banana. Even though it looks scary, its spikes do not sting.

**Longest insect**
This was a stick insect called *Phryganistria chinensis* from Chengdu in China. It was an astonishing 25.19 in (64 cm) in length. The measurement was taken with the insect's front and back legs fully outstretched.

**Longest beetle**
The Hercules beetle is an impressive creature from the rainforests of Central and South America. It can reach 6.7 in (17 cm) in length and lift 17 lb (8 kg)—that is 80 times its own weight.

A **SAHARAN SILVER ANT** COULD BEAT ANY OTHER ANT IN A RACE. IT COVERS 108 TIMES ITS OWN BODY LENGTH PER SECOND.

THE BULLDOG ANT IS THE WORLD'S MOST DANGEROUS ANT. ITS **TOXIC** STING CAN KILL A HUMAN.

THE GIANT BORNEO CARPENTER BEE GIVES THE MOST PAINFUL STING OF ANY BEE.

**Highest jumper**
The common froghopper is a champion jumper. It can jump 27.5 in (70 cm) in the air, which is higher than a flea.

**FAST FACTS**

1. Red fire ant — Small electric shock
3. Velvet ant — Hot oil on hand
4. Bullet ant — Foot with nail in it on hot coals

American Dr. Justin Schmidt has invented an index to measure and describe the pain of stings caused by various insects. The greatest pain is rated as 4.

**Longest proboscis**
The Wallace's sphinx moth's proboscis (or drinking tube) can reach up to 11.2 in (28.5 cm). It feeds on nectar stored at the bottom of deep flowers.

**Insects have developed** some extraordinary features to help them thrive in their environments. Whether it is growing extra-long or leaping super-high, these insects are all winners.

**Smallest insect**
These tiny fairy wasps can be seen only with a magnifying glass. They are only a fifth of a millimeter (0.007 inches) long.

**Heaviest insect**
The giant weta lives among leaves on the ground in New Zealand and weighs 0.7–1 oz (20–30 g) on average. A pregnant female, however, was found to weigh 2.4 oz (70 g).

This record-breaking bug was specially bred at the Insect Museum of West China in 2017.

THE **LEAF CUTTER ANT** IS EARTH'S STRONGEST ANT. IT CAN LIFT LEAVES UP TO 50 TIMES ITS OWN BODY WEIGHT!

THE EXTINCT GIGANTIC TITAN ANT WAS THE LARGEST ANT EVER, AT **2.4** IN (6 CM) LONG. IT HAD WINGS, TOO, THAT WERE UP TO 5.9 IN (15 CM) WIDE.

**THE YELLOW-BELLIED SEA SNAKE SWIMS FASTEST, AT 3 FT (1 M) PER SECOND ...**

**Longest snake**
This honor falls to the reticulated python. There are reports of it reaching lengths of 32 ft (10 m), though it's usually nearer to 23 ft (7 m).

**Longest fangs**
Lurking in the rainforests and savannas of central Africa, the Gaboon viper has the longest fangs of all snakes—they are 2 in (5 cm) long.

**... Most venomous**
Look out for this snake, because its bite is lethal. The inland taipan lives in Australia and is the most venomous snake in the world; just one bite could kill 100 adult men.

**Smallest snake**
This tiny snake is only 4 in (10 cm) long and as thin as a spaghetti strand. It is called a Barbados threadsnake.

**1,100** THE ANTIGUAN RACER WAS THE WORLD'S RAREST SNAKE IN 1995. NOW THERE ARE OVER 1,100.

**PARADISE FLYING SNAKES CAN GLIDE UP TO 330 FT (100 M) BETWEEN TREE BRANCHES.**

... AND IT HAS THE WIDEST RANGE, AROUND THE PACIFIC AND INDIAN OCEANS.

# SUPER SNAKES

Some snakes are **many feet long**, while others can give a **deadly bite** with their **needlelike fangs**. However, most won't attack unless they are disturbed.

The **black mamba** is not actually **black**—except for the inside of its **mouth**.

**Fastest snake**
The black mamba, found in Africa, is highly venomous and can also move super fast. It has been known to reach speeds of more than 6.8 mph (11 km/h), making it a terrifying predator.

**Snakes vary in size** from pythons as thick as your forearm to noodle-thin threadsnakes. There are also fierce snakes with long fangs that can give a nasty bite.

### FAST FACTS

**The green anaconda** is the heaviest snake in the world, weighing up to 500 lb (227 kg). That's as much as two-and-a-half male red kangaroos, which weigh 198 lb (90 kg) each.

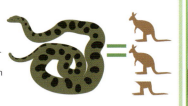

# 16,076

**THE HIMALAYAN PIT VIPER LIVES AT ALTITUDES UP TO 16,076 FT (4,900 M).**

**AUSTRALIA** IS HOME TO NINE OF THE WORLD'S TOP 10 MOST VENOMOUS SNAKES, INCLUDING THE INLAND TAIPAN.

AFRICA'S SILVERY MOLE-RAT IS THE TOOTHIEST RODENT, WITH 28 TEETH.

Burrows have separate **sleeping quarters, nurseries for the young**, and even **toilets**.

**Largest prairie dog town**
A network of prairie dog burrows in Texas covered 25,000 sq miles (65,000 sq km). That's the size of the state of West Virginia or the country of Lithuania. It was home for 400 million prairie dogs.

# RODENT RECORDS

From tiny **mouselike** jerboas to **capybaras** as big as a pig, there is a wide variety of **rodents**. Some dig vast **burrows** underground to live in and raise their young.

THE **ARCTIC GROUND SQUIRREL** HIBERNATES FOR NINE MONTHS EACH YEAR, LONGER THAN ANY OTHER RODENT.

ARGENTINA'S PATAGONIAN MARA IS THE FASTEST-MOVING RODENT, WITH A TOP SPEED OF 37 MPH (60 KM/H

# THERE ARE ABOUT SEVEN BILLION RATS IN THE WORLD—AROUND ONE PER PERSON!

**Highest-jumping rodent**
This kangaroo rat can leap up to 9 ft (2.75 m) high. It has extra-long back legs and weighs less than 4.5 oz (128 g).

**Spikiest rodent**
Porcupines have long spines called quills to protect them from predators. The quills of the North African crested porcupine can be up to 13.7 in (35 cm) long.

**Biggest rodent**
The capybara spends a lot of time in water in its South American habitat. It grows to 53 in (134 cm) long and weighs up to 145 lb (66 kg).

**Smallest rodent**
The tiny Asian Baluchistan pygmy jerboa measures just 1.7 in (4.4 cm) from its head to the start of its tail—its tail is 3 in (8 cm) long.

**Biggest ears**
With a body just 3.7 in (9.5 cm) long and ears measuring 1.5–2 in (4–5 cm) in length, the long-eared jerboa is appropriately named. It has the longest ears compared to its body of any mammal.

**Rodents are mammals** with two continuously growing teeth, which they use to eat plants and seeds. Some also have an extra-long tail to help them balance when they jump.

### BIGGEST TEETH

**The largest rodent** that has ever lived was the *Josephoartigasia monesi*. This creature, which was the size of a bull, lived during the Pliocene period (5.3–2.6 million years ago). It was about 5 ft (1.5 m) tall and 10 ft (3 m) long and had enormous incisor teeth that were 12 in (30 cm) long. It probably used its teeth for digging and fighting as well as eating.

**THE NAKED MOLE-RAT HAS THE RODENT WORLD'S LONGEST LIFE EXPECTANCY: 28 YEARS.**

**PRAIRIE DOGS USE DIFFERENT VOCAL SOUNDS TO WARN EACH OTHER OF DIFFERENT TYPES OF PREDATORS.**

**PRIMATES FIRST APPEARED ON EARTH ABOUT 65 MILLION YEARS AGO.**

**Most like humans**
Both chimpanzees and bonobos (an ape that looks very similar to the chimpanzee) share 98.7 percent of their DNA with humans.

**Smallest ape**
Though gibbons are the smallest apes—about 3.2 ft (1 m) tall—they have the longest arms in relation to their body of any animal.

**Largest ape**
The mighty Eastern gorilla is the largest of the apes. Males grow up to 6 ft (1.9 m) tall and can weigh 461 lb (209 kg).

**Most intelligent**
Studies have found that the orangutan might be the most intelligent ape. They can use a variety of tools and spend many years educating their young.

A gibbon can reach speeds of 35 mph (56 km/h) when it swings through the trees.

**Apes and monkeys are both primates,** but apes are bigger and, unlike most monkeys, do not have tails. Apes are more intelligent and more likely to use tools to get at their food. Monkeys live in all sorts of environments, including snowy ones.

THE AYE-AYE LEMUR HAS A SUPER-LONG FINGER IT USES TO TAP ON WOOD TO DETECT PREY IN THE DARK.

CHIMPANZEES LIVE ABOUT 40 YEARS. CHEETAH, THE STAR OF THE TARZAN FILMS OF THE 1930S, DIED IN 2011, AT AGE 80.

THE PATAS MONKEY, THE WORLD'S FASTEST PRIMATE, CAN RUN AT 34 MPH (55 KM/H).

**Loudest monkey**
The howler monkey makes deep, booming calls that can be heard up to 3 miles (5 km) away.

**Smallest monkey**
A pygmy marmoset weighs only 3–5 oz (85–140 g), making it the smallest monkey.

**Longest nose**
The proboscis monkey has the longest nose (or proboscis). It is so long that the monkey has to push it aside to eat.

**Largest monkey**
The mandrill is the largest monkey, growing up to 31 in (80 cm) tall and weighing 73 lb (33 kg). However, it is nowhere near as big as the largest ape. It is the most distinctive monkey, though, with its red nose and blue face patches.

**Most northerly monkey**
The Japanese macaque lives the farthest north of any nonhuman primate, dwelling in snowy landscapes where temperatures can reach as low as 5°F (–15°C).

# PRIZE-WINNING
# PRIMATES

Our nearest relatives, **apes and monkeys** are **intelligent** animals, but which are the largest, the **loudest**, or the most like us?

**4,300**
FOSSILS FOUND IN 2017 SHOWED THAT CHIMPANZEES WERE USING STONE TOOLS 4,300 YEARS AGO IN AFRICA.

**MOST PRIMATES LIVE IN TROPICAL AREAS OF AFRICA, ASIA, CENTRAL AMERICA, AND SOUTH AMERICA.**

THE PLATYPUS AND ECHIDNA ARE UNUSUAL MAMMALS BECAUSE THEY LAY EGGS.

# BIG BABIES

From the **tallest newborns** to **super-size litters** and long **pregnancies**, discover these record-breaking **mammal** babies.

A **newborn giraffe** is on its feet within **one hour** of being **born**.

**All the babies here are placental mammals**, which means that they develop fully inside their mother. Marsupial mammals, such as kangaroos, have young that continue to develop in their mother's pouch after birth.

**Tallest baby**
A newborn giraffe is 6 ft (1.8 m) tall—the same height as an average adult man.

**Most babies**
A female rabbit in the wild can have 360 kits in her lifetime, up to 14 in each litter.

**Biggest litter**
Tenrecs—small, hedgehog-like animals from Madagascar—have up to 32 babies in one litter. The average litter size is 18.

**GIRAFFES** GIVE BIRTH STANDING UP. CALVES DROP 6 FT (2 M) TO THE GROUND.

**GIANT PANDA CUBS** ARE BORN PINK WITH FINE FUR THAT TURNS BLACK AND WHITE AFTER ABOUT THREE WEEKS.

YOUNG ORANGUTANS STAY WITH THEIR MOTHERS FOR SIX TO EIGHT YEARS.

### WEIGHTY WHALES

The heaviest newborn of all is the 23 ft (7 m) long blue whale, weighing in at 6,000 lb (2,700 kg). This is 60 times lighter than its mother: in fact, it's the same weight as her tongue.

**Smallest baby compared to mother**
At birth, a panda cub is 900 times smaller than its mother by weight. A human baby is about 20 times smaller than its mom.

**Longest childhood**
A female orangutan is looked after by its mother for eight years, the longest childhood in the animal kingdom.

**Longest pregnancy**
A baby elephant takes 22 months (640–660 days) to develop inside its mother. That's more than twice as long as a human baby's 9 months (280 days).

MALE SEAHORSES AND SEA DRAGONS CARRY AND HATCH EGGS FERTILIZED BY THE FEMALE.

BABY ELEPHANTS ARE BORN STANDING 3 FT (1 M) TALL AND WEIGHING ABOUT 220 LB (100 KG).

THE GREEK WORD FOR MAYFLY, *EPHEMEROPTERA*, MEANS "SHORT-LIVED WITH WINGS."

# LONGEST LIFE SPANS

Life can be fleeting or long-lasting in the **animal kingdom**. Some creatures pack a lifetime into a **day**, while others can survive for **centuries**.

**Mayfly (1 day)**
Some mayflies live for a few hours or days, but females of one species live up to five minutes—just long enough to mate and lay eggs.

**Asian elephant (86 years)**
Apart from humans, the longest-living land mammal is the mighty elephant. An Asian elephant named Lin Wang lived to be 86 years old in Taipei Zoo, Taiwan.

**Human (up to 122 years)**
We are the longest-living land-dwelling mammals on Earth, with the oldest person ever reaching 122 years.

**Bowhead whale (more than 200 years)**
Bowhead whales are the longest-living mammals, capable of reaching 211 years of age.

**Koi carp (226 years)**
This popular pet species can live a long life. A koi carp named Hanako was reported to be 226 years old when she died in 1977.

**Aldabra giant tortoise (255 years)**
The oldest reptile ever recorded lived in Kolkata, India. The Aldabra giant tortoise named Adwaita reached 255 years of age. He died in 2006.

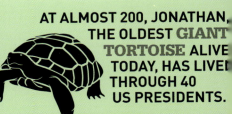

**50** IN THE WILD, ASIAN ELEPHANTS LIVE FOR AN AVERAGE OF **50** YEARS BUT HAVE BEEN KNOWN TO REACH 70 YEARS.

AT ALMOST 200, JONATHAN, THE OLDEST **GIANT TORTOISE** ALIVE TODAY, HAS LIVED THROUGH 40 US PRESIDENTS.

MAYFLIES HAVE NO MOUTH PARTS BECAUSE THEY DON'T LIVE LONG ENOUGH TO EAT.   125

**Naked mole-rat (28 years)**
This strange-looking underground rodent from East Africa is the longest-living rodent, capable of reaching 28 years of age.

**Royal python (47.5 years)**
The longest-living snake is the nonvenomous royal python from Africa. It is a popular pet and can live for more than 47 years in captivity.

**There are big differences in the life spans of animals**, though they all face the same challenges to survive. They must hunt for food, avoid predators, and find a mate in order to produce the next generation.

30

**Laysan albatross (71+ years)**
The oldest bird recorded in the wild is aged at least 71—a Laysan albatross named Wisdom.

50

**Termite queen (50 years)**
A termite queen can live for 50 years, making her the world's longest-living insect.

60

**Greenland shark (392 years)**
Researchers have found a Greenland shark possibly aged about 392 years old, making her the longest-living vertebrate.

**Icelandic clam (507 years)**
Meet Hafrún, the Icelandic clam aged 507 years old. This ocean quahog holds the record for the longest-living mollusk.

**Deep sea sponges, including *Monorhaphis chuni*, are estimated to live for 11,000 years.**

500

11,000

**MOST KOI CARP LIVE FOR ABOUT 40 YEARS AND THEIR FISH SCALES FEATURE GROWTH RINGS, LIKE RINGS ON A TREE.**

**SCIENTISTS DISCOVERED BOWHEAD WHALES HAVE A SPECIAL GENE THAT HELPS PROTECT THEM FROM SERIOUS ILLNESSES LIKE CANCER.**

POLAR BEAR FUR LOOKS WHITE BUT IS TRANSLUCENT—AND THEIR SKIN IS BLACK.

# Animal data

## THE BIG SLEEP

**DALL'S PORPOISE** SLEEP VERY LITTLE

**LITTLE BROWN BAT**

THE **LITTLE BROWN BAT** SLEEPS FOR ALMOST **20 HOURS A DAY.** SOME ANIMALS, SUCH AS **DALL'S PORPOISE,** APPEAR **NOT TO SLEEP AT ALL.**

**19.9 HOURS**

THE **EDIBLE DORMOUSE** HAS THE **LONGEST HIBERNATION** OF ANY ANIMAL: MORE THAN 11 MONTHS OF THE YEAR.

## miniMALS

- **SMALLEST MAMMAL:** KITTI'S HOG-NOSED BAT, 1.2 IN (30 MM) BODY LENGTH
- **SMALLEST REPTILE:** BROOKESIA NANA CHAMELEON, 0.86 IN (21.9 MM) FROM NOSE TO TAIL
- **SMALLEST AMPHIBIAN:** PAEDOPHRYNE AMAUENSIS FROG, 0.3 IN (7.7 MM) LONG
- **SMALLEST INVERTEBRATE:** TINY AQUATIC CREATURES CALLED ROTIFERS ARE AMONG THE SMALLEST ANIMALS. THE TINIEST IS 0.002 IN (0.05 MM) LONG.

## IT'S A KNOCKOUT

**Peacock mantis shrimps** have one of the **fastest and most powerful punches** made by any animal, striking with a force **2,500 times their own body weight** in less than 800 microseconds (0.0008 seconds). They use **special clubs** on their front legs to **smash the shells of crabs** for food. The force of their **punch is so great** that it has been known to **smash the glass of an aquarium**.

POW

**OCTOPUS AND HORSESHOE CRAB** BLOOD IS BLUE BECAUSE IT HAS COPPER IN IT RATHER THAN IRON.

**HORNED LIZARDS** IN THE US AND MEXICO CAN SHOOT BLOOD FROM THEIR EYES TO SCARE AWAY PREDATORY COYOTES AND WOLVES.

TIGERS HAVE THE SAME PATTERN OF STRIPES ON BOTH THEIR FUR AND THEIR SKIN.

# DEADLIEST CREATURES

**GIANT ARMADILLOS HAVE THE LARGEST CLAWS:** ONE CURVED FRONT CLAW IS UP TO 8 IN (20.3 CM) LONG.

**ANOPHELES MOSQUITOES ARE THE DEADLIEST ANIMALS OF ALL:** FEMALE MOSQUITOES SPREAD MALARIA THROUGH THEIR BITES, KILLING HUNDREDS OF THOUSANDS OF PEOPLE EVERY YEAR.

**SPERM WHALES HAVE THE BIGGEST TEETH OF ANY PREDATOR:** UP TO 8 IN (20 CM) LONG.

**ELECTRIC EELS HAVE THE STRONGEST ELECTRICAL DISCHARGE:** EACH SHOCK CAN PROVIDE 600 VOLTS TO ITS PREY OR OTHER PREDATORS. THAT'S NEARLY THREE TIMES THE VOLTAGE PROVIDED BY A HOUSEHOLD ELECTRIC SOCKET.

# MEGA MUNCHERS

The **blue whale** eats the **most food of any animal**: around **6 tons of krill**—or **40 million** of the **tiny sea crustaceans**—every day. That's **about 4–5 percent** of its **body weight**.

# LONGEST ANIMAL

A **bootlace worm** measuring more than **180 ft (55 m) long** washed up from the **North Sea** onto the coast of **Scotland, UK, in 1864.** Stretched out, it could wrap around the **edge of these pages** more than **80 times**.

**Eurasian pygmy shrews** eat **125 percent** of their **body weight a day**: that's up to **0.18 oz (5 g) of food a day**.

**JELLYFISH AND CORAL HAVE NO BLOOD. INSTEAD, OXYGEN REACHES THEIR CELLS VIA GAS EXCHANGE.**

**THE ANTARCTIC BLACKFIN ICEFISH IS THE ONLY VERTEBRATE WITH WHITE BLOOD. IT ALSO HAS SEE-THROUGH BONES.**

**DIPLODOCUS WAS DOUBLE THE WEIGHT OF AN AFRICAN ELEPHANT.**

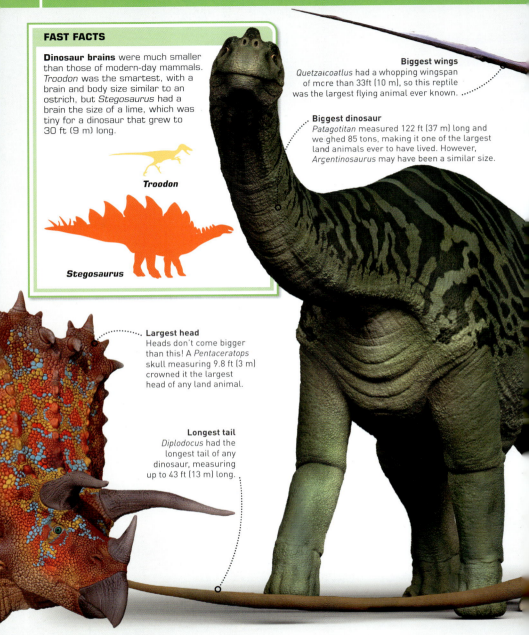

### FAST FACTS

**Dinosaur brains** were much smaller than those of modern-day mammals. *Troodon* was the smartest, with a brain and body size similar to an ostrich, but *Stegosaurus* had a brain the size of a lime, which was tiny for a dinosaur that grew to 30 ft (9 m) long.

*Troodon*

*Stegosaurus*

**Biggest wings**
*Quetzalcoatlus* had a whopping wingspan of more than 33ft (10 m), so this reptile was the largest flying animal ever known.

**Biggest dinosaur**
*Patagotitan* measured 122 ft (37 m) long and weighed 85 tons, making it one of the largest land animals ever to have lived. However, *Argentinosaurus* may have been a similar size.

**Largest head**
Heads don't come bigger than this! A *Pentaceratops* skull measuring 9.8 ft (3 m) crowned it the largest head of any land animal.

**Longest tail**
*Diplodocus* had the longest tail of any dinosaur, measuring up to 43 ft (13 m) long.

**PENTACERATOPS** HAD FIVE "HORNS" AND A FRILL ON ITS HEAD, POSSIBLY TO SCARE RIVALS AND ATTRACT MATES.

**DIPLODOCUS** USED ITS LONG, POWERFUL TAIL AS A WEAPON TO SWIPE AWAY PREDATORS WITH A SINGLE FLICK!

QUETZALCOATLUS COULD TAKE OFF BECAUSE ITS BONES WERE HOLLOW AND LIGHT.

# AWESOME DINOSAURS

**Size matters** for dinosaurs. Although these extinct reptiles lived more than **66 million years ago**, they are still the **largest creatures** to have ever walked the Earth.

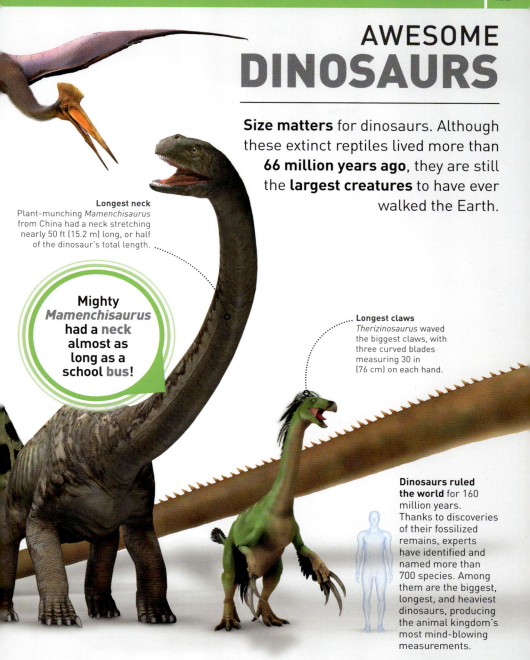

**Longest neck**
Plant-munching *Mamenchisaurus* from China had a neck stretching nearly 50 ft (15.2 m) long, or half of the dinosaur's total length.

Mighty *Mamenchisaurus* had a **neck** almost as long as a school **bus**!

**Longest claws**
*Therizinosaurus* waved the biggest claws, with three curved blades measuring 30 in (76 cm) on each hand.

**Dinosaurs ruled the world** for 160 million years. Thanks to discoveries of their fossilized remains, experts have identified and named more than 700 species. Among them are the biggest, longest, and heaviest dinosaurs, producing the animal kingdom's most mind-blowing measurements.

T HAD THE BIGGEST CLAWS OF ANY CREATURE EVER, BUT THERIZINOSAURUS JSED THEM ONLY TO EAR AND EAT PLANTS.

MAMENCHISAURUS'S HUGE NECK WAS HELD UP BY 18 OR 19 BONES SURROUNDED BY HOLLOW SPACES TO LIGHTEN THE LOAD.

A FOSSILIZED DINOSAUR PRESERVED ON HER NEST OF EGGS WAS FOUND IN CHINA.

# THE DINOSAUR TAIL CONTINUES...

From the **first to the fastest**, and the **latest to the longest-lived**, these dinosaurs have all broken records. However, the story is not finished—**fossils** are still being found, bringing new information and new records.

*Diplodocus* had a long digestive system to help it digest its **fibrous, leafy diet.**

**First dinosaur**
Fossils of this small, dog-size dinosaur, named *Nyasasaurus parringtoni*, were uncovered in Tanzania. They have been dated at 243 million years old, which is more than 10 million years earlier than any other dinosaur fossils.

 THE WORLD'S BIGGEST DINOSAUR MUSEUM, SHANDONG TIANYU MUSEUM OF NATURE IN CHINA, HAS **1,100 SPECIMENS.**

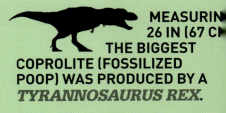 MEASURING 26 IN (67 CM) THE BIGGEST COPROLITE (FOSSILIZED POOP) WAS PRODUCED BY A *TYRANNOSAURUS REX*.

PIONEERING FOSSIL HUNTER MARY ANNING FOUND THE FIRST *ICHTHYOSAUR* IN 1811.

**The story of dinosaurs** still presents us with some puzzles. Here are some of the earliest dinosaurs that have been discovered as well as some that survived for the longest.

### FAST FACTS

**A record-breaking** collection of dinosaur eggs is housed at the Heyuan Museum in Guangdong Province, China. More than 10,000 eggs are on display dating from the late Cretaceous period, which was approximately 89–65 million years ago.

**Longest-lived dinosaur**
*Diplodocus*, like other sauropods (long-necked, plant-eating dinosaurs), had a life as long as its neck. Sauropods were among the longest-lived dinosaurs, surviving for up to 80 years.

**First-named dinosaur**
*Megalosaurus* was the first dinosaur to be named. In 1824, a British geologist, Reverend William Buckland, found the fossil remains and gave the dinosaur its name, which means "great lizard."

**Most recent dinosaur**
This dinosaur was a survivor. Fossils of the plant-eating hadrosaurs have been dated at 64.5 million years. If the date is right, this means it survived the huge asteroid that killed off the large dinosaurs and was still around 700,000 years later.

**Fastest dinosaur**
The *ornithomimids* were the speediest dinosaurs. They looked a bit like big birds with feathers, beaks, and long legs. *Struthiomimus* had a top speed of 45 mph (72 km/h).

**SHANDONG IN CHINA IS THE WORLD'S BIGGEST FOSSIL SITE, WITH 7,600 FOUND SO FAR.**

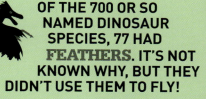

OF THE 700 OR SO NAMED DINOSAUR SPECIES, 77 HAD **FEATHERS**. IT'S NOT KNOWN WHY, BUT THEY DIDN'T USE THEM TO FLY!

# PREHISTORIC WONDERS

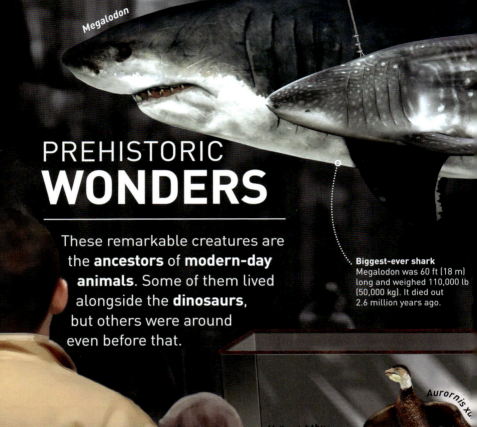

These remarkable creatures are the **ancestors** of **modern-day animals**. Some of them lived alongside the **dinosaurs**, but others were around even before that.

*Megalodon*

**Biggest-ever shark**
Megalodon was 60 ft (18 m) long and weighed 110,000 lb (50,000 kg). It died out 2.6 million years ago.

*Haikouichthys*

**Earliest fish**
This animal lived about 530 million years ago. It is called *Haikouichthys* and is thought to be the ancestor of most vertebrates living today.

*Aurornis xui*

**Earliest bird**
*Aurornis xui* lived about 160 million years ago. Fossils show that it had feathers and was the size of a pheasant.

**WOOLLY MAMMOTH** PACKS WERE AROUND 15-STRONG, WITH A FEMALE LEADER.

**THE POWERHOUSE *PARACERATHERIUM*** WAS SO TALL THAT EACH OF ITS THIGH BONES WAS 5 FT (1.5 M) LONG.

**MIGHTY MEGALODON ATE ABOUT 2,500 LB (1,130 KG) OF FOOD A DAY.**

**Biggest shark today**
The largest shark alive today is the whale shark. On average, whale sharks are 32.8 ft (10 m) long.

*Whale shark*

**Biggest land mammal**
The *Paraceratherium* was the largest land mammal and ancestor of the modern-day rhinoceros (though it didn't have a horn). It weighed 44,000 lb (20,000 kg) and was 18 ft (5.5 m) tall.

*Paraceratherium*

### FAST FACTS

**Modern elephants** are closely related to extinct mammoths—they share a common ancestor. Woolly mammoths lived in Russia, especially Siberia, and North America until 4,300 years ago. The mastodons are more distantly related to elephants and roamed North America until 10,000 years ago.

American mastodon | Woolly mammoth | African elephant

*White rhinoceros*

**These are some of the ancestors** of modern-day animals. They look a bit like animals we know, though some were much, much bigger.

*Hylonomus*

**Earliest reptile**
Discovered in the mid-19th century, *Hylonomus* lived around 312 million years ago. It was typically around 7.9 in (20 cm) long and would probably have looked very similar to modern lizard species.

**Biggest rhino**
The white rhinoceros is the largest of the five rhino species and the second-largest land mammal; African and Asian elephants are the largest.

**METASPRIGGINA WALCOTTI, ONE OF THE EARLIEST VERTEBRATE CREATURES, SWAM IN THE OCEANS 500 MILLION YEARS AGO. IT WAS JUST 2 IN (5 CM) LONG.**

**THE GLYPTODON IS THE ANCESTOR OF THE ARMADILLO. IT LIVED 3 MILLION YEARS AGO AND WAS THE SIZE OF A CAR.**

**TYRANNOSAURUS REX'S SERRATED TEETH COULD BITE THROUGH SOLID BONE!**

**The skull**
Stan's is the best-preserved *T. rex* skull ever found and includes 58 daggerlike teeth.

A puncture **wound** in Stan's skull means he was probably **bitten** by another *T. rex*.

**Stan, the *Tyrannosaurus rex*,** stands guard in the Rockefeller Center in New York City, just before his auction in 2020. It took more than 30,000 hours of work to excavate him and piece his bones back together.

# A *TYRANNOSAURUS* NAMED STAN

In 1987, in South Dakota, amateur **paleontologist Stan Sacrison** spotted the fossils of a *Tyrannosaurus rex*. It was named Stan after him, and it turned out to be a record breaker.

 **STRONG LEG MUSCLES ALLOWED *T. REX* TO REACH TOP SPEEDS OF 15 MPH (25 KM/H).**

ALTHOUGH STAN IS NAMED AFTER THE MAN WHO FOUND HIM, HIS SEX ISN'T KNOWN. HE IS PROBABLY MALE, BASED ON HIS PELVIS SIZE.

THE BITE OF *T. REX* WAS 10 TIMES MORE POWERFUL THAN A MODERN-DAY ALLIGATOR.

## FAST FACTS

**The titanosaurs were a group of sauropods (plant eaters)**, which included the largest and heaviest dinosaurs ever found. *Patagotitan* is a titanosaur that was discovered in Argentina in 2012. Its thigh bone is the largest fossil ever discovered, measuring 7.8 ft (2.4 m) long. The fossils are on display in the American Museum of Natural History, New York.

*Patagotitan* 122 ft (37 m) long

**Stan** 40 ft (12.2 m) long

**Human** 6 ft (1.8 m) tall

*Patagotitan* thigh bone 7.8 ft (2.4 m) long

**Large and almost complete**
Stan measures 40 ft (12.2 m) from snout to tail and contains 188 bones. He is one of the most complete *T. rex* skeletons ever found.

**Most valuable**
This *T. rex* skeleton is the world's most valuable. At an auction in 2020, it was sold to The Natural History Museum Abu Dhabi, in the United Arab Emirates, for $31.8 million (£25.08 million).

A LIFE-SIZE REPLICA OF **STAN** IS ON DISPLAY AT THE "ZOORASSIC WORLD" ATTRACTION IN DUBLIN ZOO IN THE REPUBLIC OF IRELAND.

STAN WAS ABOUT **20** AT HIS TIME OF DEATH. SOME EXPERTS THINK THE CAUSE MAY HAVE BEEN A FIGHT WITH ANOTHER *T. REX*.

HYPERION IS NAMED AFTER THE GREEK GOD OF HEAVENLY LIGHT.

# TREE-
# MENDOUS

The first trees grew on Earth about **385 million years ago**. Today there are 3 trillion trees providing a **life-support system** for our planet, giving **oxygen and shelter** for animals, including humans.

**Trees are natural wonders**, whether growing in forests or alone on mountainsides. Some trees have survived for thousands of years and others have grown to dizzying heights.

**Hyperion** is 75.5 ft (23 m) taller than the **Statue of Liberty.**

**Hyperion is such a giant** that the tiny human figures in its branches look like insects on a garden plant!

**Tallest tree**
The world's tallest tree is the mighty Hyperion, in Redwood National Park, California, standing 380 (116 m) tall when it was measured in 2006. Very few people know the exact location of this record breaker.

### FAST FACTS

A study in 2015 estimated that there were 3 trillion trees on Earth. Russia has the most trees with 642 billion, followed by Canada (318 billion), Brazil (302 billion), and the US (228 billion).

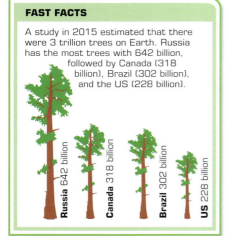

**THE WORLD'S SLOWEST-GROWING TREE IS A WHITE CEDAR IN CANADA THAT TOOK 155 YEARS TO GROW TO JUST 4 IN (10.2 CM)!**

THE EXACT LOCATION OF METHUSELAH IS A CLOSELY GUARDED SECRET.

**Oldest tree**
The oldest trees still growing today are the bristlecone pines in the White Mountains of California. Their growth rings reveal that they are more than 9,000 years old.

**Fastest-growing tree**
China's empress tree is the world's fastest-growing tree. In one year it grows 20 ft (6 m) in height; that's about 12 in (30 cm) every few weeks. The empress breaks another record, too—it produces at least three times more oxygen than any other type of tree.

**Rarest tree**
There is only one *Pennantia baylisiana* growing anywhere in the wild. This solitary tree can be found on one of the Three Kings Islands off New Zealand.

**Widest tree**
The world's widest tree is *El Arbol del Tule*, a Montezuma cypress in Mexico, reaching more than 46 ft (14 m) across. It was mistaken for a group of trees at first because it is so wide. It would take 30 people with their arms outstretched to reach around it.

**Oldest root system** Old Tjikko is a Norway spruce in the Fulufjället Mountains of Sweden. It has a root system that is about 9,550 years old.

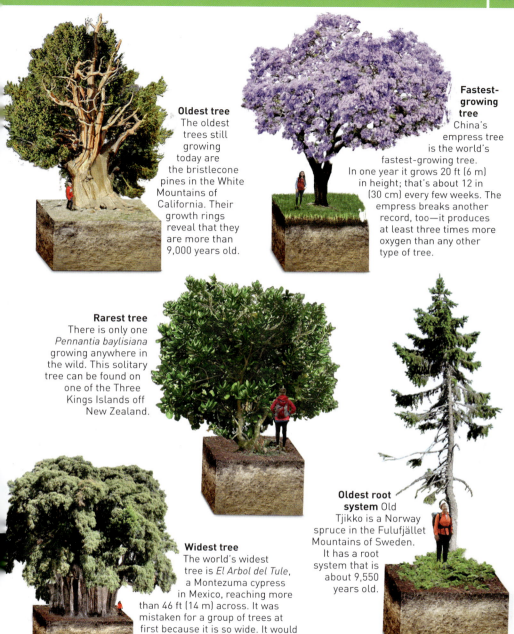

**NEW ZEALAND'S** LAST *PENNANTIA BAYLISIANA* ONLY SURVIVES BECAUSE IT'S ON A STEEP SLOPE THAT HUNGRY GOATS CAN'T REACH!

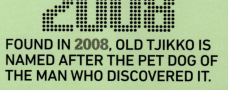

FOUND IN 2008, OLD TJIKKO IS NAMED AFTER THE PET DOG OF THE MAN WHO DISCOVERED IT.

THE HUGELY EXPENSIVE SHENZHEN NONGKE ORCHID IS EDIBLE!

# FLOWER
# POWER

Flowers have been growing on Earth for around **175 million years**. Explore these blooms and discover nature's most impressive flowers, from the **biggest blossom** to the **stinkiest flowers**.

**Biggest flower**
The world's most gigantic flower is Indonesia's *Rafflesia arnoldii*, which can grow to 3.3 ft (1 m) wide and weigh 22 lb (10 kg).

**Both the largest and tallest flowers** are among the stinkiest! *Rafflesia arnoldii* and titan arum are called "corpse flowers" because they smell of rotten meat.

**Short-lived flowers**
South America's kadupul cactus flower is a rare sight. White flowers with a beautiful scent appear only at night and are dead by morning. An orchid called *Dendrobium appendiculatum* opens for only five minutes.

**RAFFLESIA ARNOLDII** GROWS ONLY ON BORNEO AND SUMATRA, ISLANDS ON THE EQUATOR.

WHEN A TITAN ARUM AT KEW GARDENS BLOOMED IN 1926, THE **POLICE** WERE CALLED TO CONTROL THE CROWDS THAT CAME TO SEE IT!

PUYA RAIMONDII IS NAMED "QUEEN OF THE ANDES" FOR ITS MOUNTAINOUS HABITAT. | 139

**Tallest, smelliest flowering structure**
The spike of a titan arum grows up to 9.8 ft (3 m) tall and is covered with tiny flowers. It grows in the steamy rainforests of Indonesia.

**Slowest-growing**
The Bolivian bromeliad *Puya raimondii* is the ultimate late developer. Flowers first appear between 80 and 150 years after this plant starts growing!

### FAST FACTS

**The world's tiniest flower** blooms on the super-small *Wolffia globosa*, more commonly known as the Asian watermeal. Found floating in streams and ponds, the whole plant measures only 0.02 in (0.6 mm) long and 0.01 in (0.3 mm) wide—about the same size as a grain of salt.

**Oldest flowers**
Some of the oldest-known flowering plants found as fossils lived in water, such as this *Archaefructus*, which grew in China at least 125 million years ago.

**Most expensive flowering plant**
The Shenzhen Nongke orchid took eight years to produce in a laboratory before being sold at auction in 2005 for a record-breaking $202,000 (£144,000).

THE **KADUPUL CACTUS** HAS BEEN USED FOR CENTURIES IN ASIA TO TREAT AILMENTS AND ILLNESSES.

DESPITE ITS HEFTY **PRICE TAG,** THE SHENZEN NONGKE ORCHID FLOWERS ONLY EVERY 4–5 YEARS!

IF EATEN, THE ELEPHANT CREEPER'S SEEDS CAN CAUSE HALLUCINATIONS.

# LEAFY
# LEGENDS

It's not only a plant's **flowers** that attract attention. Leaves can also grow to **extraordinary lengths** and survive in **water**, in the **desert**, or at the very tops of trees.

**Biggest floating leaf**
*Victoria amazonica* water lily leaves can reach 10 ft (3 m) in diameter. They are so strong, they could support the weight of a small child.

## FAST FACTS

**Coconut trees** are probably the most useful trees in the world. Their leaves are woven into baskets, wood is used for building and carved into utensils, fiber is turned into ropes and matting, coconuts are eaten, and their oil is used as flavoring and in cosmetics.

- Baskets
- Drinks
- Ice cream
- Rope
- Shampoo
- Buildings
- Utensils

**BAMBOO** IS SUPER-STRONG AND FLEXIBLE, SO IT IS USED TO MAKE HOMES AND SCAFFOLDING IN PARTS OF AFRICA, ASIA, AND SOUTH AMERICA.

HUGE *VICTORIA AMAZONICA* WATER LILIES WERE NAMED IN HONOR OF QUEEN VICTORIA.

THE ELEPHANT CACTUS HAS A STURDY, THICK STEM—LIKE AN ELEPHANT'S LEG!

**Longest vine**
This twisting vine is an elephant creeper, a type of liana (a woody vine that grows up from the ground and wraps itself around trees). It was claimed that one specimen in India reached 4,900 ft (1.5 km) in length.

**Tallest living cactus**
This is a species of *cardón*, or elephant cactus, growing in Mexico's Sonoran Desert. It tops 63 ft (19.2 m)—that's taller than 10 men standing on each other's shoulders.

**Fastest-growing plant**
Bamboos include some of the fastest-growing plants. One species has been recorded growing 36 in (91 cm) in a day—so fast you can actually see it. In a year, it grows 1,090 ft (332.38 m).

**Longest leaf**
The plant with the longest leaf is the *Raphia regalis*, a type of raffia palm with leaves that can grow up to 82 ft (25 m) long—that's taller than the tree's 69 ft (21 m) height.

**Most poisonous plant**
The seeds of the castor bean contain ricin, a deadly toxin that is 12,000 times more poisonous than rattlesnake venom.

**Plants can thrive** in all sorts of environments. Their leaves are their food factories, absorbing light and producing sugar to give the plant energy to grow. The bigger the leaf, the more food it can make.

THE OIL FROM CASTOR SEEDS HAS MANY USES, AS MEDICINE, LAMP FUEL, MAKEUP, A LAXATIVE, AND AS VERMIN REPELLENT!

SAP FROM THE RAPHIA REGALIS TRUNK CAN BE EXTRACTED AND BREWED INTO A TYPE OF WINE.

**A GIANT PUMPKIN GROWS FROM SEED TO SUPER-SIZE FRUIT IN FIVE MONTHS.**

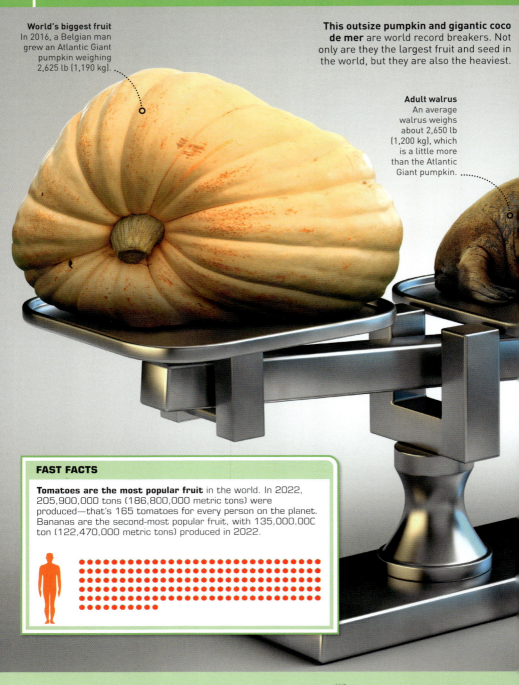

**World's biggest fruit**
In 2016, a Belgian man grew an Atlantic Giant pumpkin weighing 2,625 lb (1,190 kg).

**This outsize pumpkin and gigantic coco de mer** are world record breakers. Not only are they the largest fruit and seed in the world, but they are also the heaviest.

**Adult walrus**
An average walrus weighs about 2,650 lb (1,200 kg), which is a little more than the Atlantic Giant pumpkin.

### FAST FACTS

**Tomatoes are the most popular fruit** in the world. In 2022, 205,900,000 tons (186,800,000 metric tons) were produced—that's 165 tomatoes for every person on the planet. Bananas are the second-most popular fruit, with 135,000,000 ton (122,470,000 metric tons) produced in 2022.

**THE WINDSOR PUMPKIN REGATTA WAS A CANADIAN RACE IN WHICH ALL THE BOATS WERE MADE OF HOLLOWED-OUT GIANT PUMPKINS!**

**THE COCO DE MER TREE GROWS TO 110 FT (33.5 M), WHICH MAKES COLLECTING THEIR SEEDS A RISKY BUSINES**

AT OPTIMUM GROWTH, GIANT PUMPKINS GAIN 33 LB (15 KG) A DAY.

# FANTASTIC FRUIT

The **fruits and vegetables** we buy in the market are not this size. Gardeners grow these **monster fruits** specially to be the biggest, though the world's largest seed is a **natural wonder**.

**Border collie dog**
This dog breed's usual weight is 37 lb (17 kg), which is about the same weight as a single coco de mer seed.

**The largest seed**
The coco de mer tree, which grows only on the Seychelles islands in the Indian Ocean, produces a seed that measures up to 12 in (30 cm) long and weighs about the same as a collie dog. The very biggest seeds can weigh up to 55 lb (25 kg) or one and a half collie dogs.

The **coco de mer seed** grows inside the biggest **wild fruit**—it's up to 20 in (50 cm) across.

 COCO DE MER FRUITS TAKE UP TO 10 YEARS TO RIPEN. THEIR HUGE SHELLS ARE USED TO MAKE BOWLS AND WATER CONTAINERS.

 AT THE LA TOMATINA FESTIVAL IN SPAIN, PEOPLE SPEND ALL DAY THROWING **TOMATOES** AT EACH OTHER!

IN FOLKLORE, BELLADONNA, OR DEADLY NIGHTSHADE, HELPS WITCHES FLY!

# Flora and fungi data

## COLOR CONFUSION

THERE IS NO SUCH THING AS A **BLACK FLOWER**. EVEN THE **DARKEST OF FLOWERS** ARE JUST **VERY, VERY DARK PURPLE** OR **RED**. THE PIGMENTS THAT GIVE PETALS THEIR COLOR **DON'T PRODUCE BLACK**.

THE CARIBBEAN'S **MANCHINEEL TREES** HAVE **WARNING SIGNS** ON THEM NOT TO GO NEAR.

**IF THE TREE IS BURNED,** THE SMOKE CAN BLIND A PERSON.

**EATING THE APPLELIKE FRUIT** CAUSES DEATH BY VOMITING AND DIARRHEA.

**THE SAP BURNS THE SKIN.** EVEN RAIN DRIPPING THROUGH THE TREE ONTO A PERSON CAN CAUSE BLISTERS.

## TOXIC TREE

## TALLEST FLOWERS

**Cactus (home-grown):**
105.8 ft (32.25 m)—Peruvian apple cactus, India

**Cactus (wild):**
63 ft (19.2 m)—Cardon, Sonoran Desert, Mexico

**Sunflower:**
30 ft (9.17 m)—Germany

## PLANTS IN SPACE

**Soviet cosmonauts** on the *Salyut 7* space station grew the **first flowers in space**. The plant was *Arabidopsis*, a kind of **rock cress**, which flowered and produced seeds in **zero gravity**.

THE **COCKSCOMB PLANT'S** FLOWER LOOKS LIKE A **BRAIN** AND WAS ONCE USED TO TREAT HEADACHES.

NAMED AFTER ITS RED BLADES, JAPANESE BLOOD GRASS IS VERY FLAMMABLE AND IS THE SOURCE OF MANY **WILDFIRES**.

IN ANCIENT ATHENS, LAWBREAKERS WERE GIVEN THE DEADLY POISON HEMLOCK.

EACH FUNGUS, NO MORE THAN **0.4 IN (1 CM) TALL**, EXPLODES AND THROWS ITS **SPORES** UP TO **8.2 FT (250 CM) AWAY**; THAT IS **250 TIMES ITS BODY SIZE**.

## FASTEST FUNGUS
FOR ITS TINY SIZE, THE **HAT THROWER FUNGUS** THROWS ITS SPORES **FARTHER THAN ANY OTHER FUNGUS OR PLANT.**

## BIGGEST LIVING FUNGUS

THE **"HUMONGOUS FUNGUS"** IS A **HONEY FUNGUS** LIVING IN THE **BLUE MOUNTAINS OF OREGON,** THAT STRETCHES OVER **2,385 ACRES (965 HECTARES).**

### MOST TOXIC FUNGUS

Just **1 oz (30 g)** of the **death cap fungus**—about half of one mushroom—**can be deadly** when eaten. It's still toxic when cooked or frozen and is responsible for the highest number of fatal mushroom poisonings.

## BIGGEST SINGLE MUSHROOM

The largest fruiting body of a fungus (a mushroom) was discovered in 2010 in China. The brown, woody, rectangular *Fomitiporia ellipsoidea* was 33 in (84 cm) wide, 2 in (5 cm) thick, but 35.6 ft (10.85 m) long—nearly as long as a bus. It weighed about half a ton.

36 FT (11 M) LONG

35.6 FT (10.85 M) LONG

**VENUS FLYTRAP** LIVES UP TO ITS NAME BY CATCHING FLIES IN ITS SNAPPING "JAWS" AND DIGESTING THEM FOR DINNER!

WHITE BANEBERRY, OR "DOLL'S EYE," HAS A BLACK DOT ON ITS BERRIES THAT MAKES THEM LOOK LIKE **EYEBALLS.**

# Out of this world

Beyond our planet lies infinite space, and the vast nature of the universe means that there is always more to explore. Astronauts and astronomers seek new planets, moons, stars, asteroids, and galaxies in the ultimate challenge to discover the biggest, best, and brightest of our cosmos.

**A close-up of Buzz Aldrin's bootprint** in the lunar soil, taken on July 21, 1969, during the Apollo 11 mission—the first to land on the moon. Earlier in the day, Aldrin's fellow US astronaut Neil Armstrong had become the first man in history to walk on the moon. As he did so, he famously said: "That's one small step for man, one giant leap for mankind."

NASA'S HUBBLE SPACE TELESCOPE IS NAMED AFTER ASTRONOMER EDWIN HUBBLE.

# SPACE RECORDS

In the vast expanse of **outer space**, are things **bigger**, **brighter**, and **colder** than anything experienced on Earth?

**Considering the size of the universe**, there ought to be a lot of space records. However, our knowledge of space is limited; we have discovered only a tiny fraction of the universe. It may be that there are bigger and better things out there. Watch this space!

**Dark matter in space** can't be seen, but, according to NASA, it makes up 27 percent of the mass of the universe. Visible matter makes up less than 5 percent. The rest is dark energy.

**Biggest known nebula**
At 1,520 light-years, NGC 604, in the Messier 33 galaxy, is thought to be the biggest nebula (a dust and gas cloud). One light-year measures around 6 trillion miles (9 trillion km).

**Darkest thing**
Dark matter is invisible even when you shine a light on it. It has never been seen but is thought to exist because it would explain how parts of the universe operate.

**Brightest thing**
In 2012, scientists recorded the brightest-ever light in space. Named GRB 221009A, it came from a massive burst of gamma rays released when a dying star exploded two billion light-years from Earth.

**Biggest planet**
At 599,499 miles (964,800 km) across, HD 100546 b is the biggest-known planet. It has a radius 6.9 times bigger than that of Jupiter and takes 249.2 years to make a single orbit of its star.

THE **HUBBLE SPACE TELESCOPE** ORBITS THE EARTH—AND HAS BEEN AROUND OUR PLANET AT LEAST 175,000 TIMES SO FAR!

THE FARTHEST STAR OBSERVED BY HUBBLE IS 12 BILLION LIGHT-YEARS AWAY AND IS CALLED EARENDEL.

THE HUBBLE SPACE TELESCOPE HAS MADE MORE THAN 1.4 MILLION OBSERVATIONS. | 149

## FAST FACTS

**Telescopes in orbit** have shown us most of what we know about space. They detect different kinds of radiation given out by space bodies. The oldest telescope still in use is the Hubble Space Telescope, which detects ultraviolet, visible, and infrared light.

Hubble is 43.5 ft (13.2 m) long—about as big as a school bus.

**Launched**: April 1990
**Location**: Low Earth Orbit (340 miles/547 km above Earth). Orbits once every 95 minutes at 17,000 mph (27,300 km/h)
**Discoveries**:
• Age of universe as 13–14 billion years
• How galaxies form
• Understanding dark energy

**Hottest thing**: The universe's hottest stuff is on Earth. An experiment at the Large Hadron Collider, Switzerland, created a temperature that is about 1 billion times hotter than the surface of the sun.

**Biggest galaxy**: Alcyoneus at 16.2 million light-years wide is the largest galaxy. It was discovered in 2022 and is so far away no images of it exist yet. Until it was found, Galaxy IC 1101 (pictured) was the biggest.

**Coldest thing**: The boomerang nebula, located 5,000 light-years from Earth, is a chilly −457.9°F (−272.15°C). The nebula expands so quickly, it cools the gas inside.

**Oldest galaxy**: The 13.5-billion-year-old GLASS-z13 galaxy was found in 2022. It formed 400 million years after the Big Bang and is 100 million years older than the previous record holder, GN-Z11 (pictured).

 HD-1 IS THE FARTHEST GALAXY FROM EARTH, AN IMMENSE 13.4 BILLION LIGHT-YEARS AWAY.

 DISCOVERED IN 2012, EL GORDO IS THE LARGEST KNOWN **GALAXY CLUSTER**, A COLLECTION OF HUNDREDS OF HUGE GALAXIES.

**VENUS ROTATES VERY SLOWLY: ONE DAY THERE IS THE SAME AS 243 DAYS ON EARTH.**

**Smallest planet**
At 3,032 miles (4,879 km) across, Mercury is just over one-third the size of Earth.

**Least mass**
Mercury's mass is 18 times less than Earth's, and 5,751 times less than Jupiter, the heaviest planet.

**Hottest planet**
Although Mercury is nearer the sun, Venus has the highest average surface temperature: 867°F (464°C). Its thick atmosphere traps heat.

Mercury

Venus

**Most volcanoes**
Radar has revealed more than 1,600 volcanoes on Venus. No one knows if they are currently active, or exactly how many more there are—possibly a million.

### FAST FACTS

**Earth's iconic features** are dwarfed by those on Mars.

Olympus Mons: 13.6 miles (22 km)
Mount Everest: 5.5 miles (8.8 km)

Grand Canyon, US: 277 miles (446 km)

Valles Marineris: 2,500 miles (4,000 km)

North Polar Basin: 6,600 miles (10,600 km)

Vredefort crater, South Africa: 186 miles (300 km)

**Densest atmosphere**
Made up of 96 percent carbon dioxide, the thick atmosphere on Venus creates a crushing pressure 92 times stronger than that on Earth.

**Densest planet**
Compared to its size, the amount of material that makes up Earth makes it the densest planet.

**What makes a planet unique** can depend on its position in our solar system. For example, Venus is hotter than Mercury because Mercury is too near the sun and its atmosphere has blown away. And Earth is the only planet at the ideal distance from the sun to support life—it's neither too hot nor too cold.

ALL THE PLANETS IN THE SOLAR SYSTEM WERE NAMED AFTER ROMAN AND GREEK GODS AND GODDESSES, WITH THE EXCEPTION OF **EARTH**.

NAMED AFTER THE **ROMAN GOD OF WAR**, MARS IS ALSO CALLED "THE RED PLANET" BECAUSE ITS SURFACE IS BLOOD RED.

MEASURING 7,932 MILES (12,765 KM) WIDE, EARTH IS THE BIGGEST ROCKY PLANET.

# ROCKY PLANETS

Mercury, Venus, Earth, and Mars—known as the rocky planets—are all similar in composition, but their **size** and **position** in space give each one **unique** claims to fame.

Earth

Earth is the only planet known to have both life and liquid water on its surface.

**Largest mountain**
Olympus Mons is a volcano that stands 13.6 miles (22 km) above the surface of Mars, and is the highest in the solar system.

**Largest crater**
The North Polar, or Borealis, Basin covers about 40 percent of Mars. It is not known if it is an impact crater; if so, it would have been caused by an object the size of Pluto.

Mars

**Largest canyon**
Carving a path nearly one-fifth of the way around Mars, Valles Marineris is 2,500 miles (4,000 km) long.

VENUS WAS NAMED AFTER THE ROMAN GODDESS OF BEAUTY AND IS THE BRIGHTEST PLANET IN THE SOLAR SYSTEM AS SEEN FROM EARTH.

MERCURY, THE QUICK-FOOTED MESSENGER OF THE GODS, GAVE HIS NAME TO THE FASTEST-ORBITING PLANET.

### SNAP-HAPPY *CURIOSITY*

***Curiosity* is a car-size rover** that was designed to explore Mars as part of NASA's Mars Science Laboratory Mission. Launched on November 26, 2011, it landed on Mars on August 5, 2012, and has continued to perform scientific experiments ever since. The rover holds a unique claim to fame: it took the first-ever selfie on another planet.

THE MIGHTY PLANET JUPITER IS NAMED AFTER THE KING OF THE ROMAN GODS.

# JUPITER
# THE GIANT

Jupiter is the **heavyweight king** of the planets, holding **more records** than any other planet in the solar system.

### Strongest gravitational pull
The more mass an object has, the stronger its gravitational pull on other objects. Jupiter's gravity is about 2.5 times stronger than Earth's: if you jump 39 in (1 m) high on Earth's surface, the same jump would lift you only 15.5 in (39.5 cm) on Jupiter.

### Biggest planet
Jupiter measures 88,846 miles (142,984 km) across its widest point (the equator)—that's 11 times the diameter of Earth. Its volume is 343,382,767,518,322 cu miles (1,431,281,810,739,360 cu km), or 1,321 times that of Earth.

**Jupiter is the biggest** of the gas giants—the four planets made mostly of gas and liquid. All the other planets in the solar system could fit inside Jupiter, with room to spare!

THE STORM CLOUDS SURROUNDING JUPITER ARE FILLED WITH MYSTERIOUS FLASHES OF LIGHT KNOWN AS SPRITES AND ELVES.

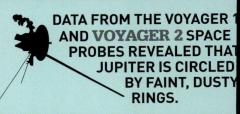

DATA FROM THE VOYAGER 1 AND VOYAGER 2 SPACE PROBES REVEALED THAT JUPITER IS CIRCLED BY FAINT, DUSTY RINGS.

THE THICK CLOUDS SWIRLING AROUND JUPITER ARE 30 MILES (50 KM) THICK. | 155

## Fastest rotation
Jupiter spins quickly, taking just 9.9 hours to make one complete rotation, even though it is so large. This gives it the shortest day of any planet.

## Greatest escape velocity
To escape the pull of Jupiter's gravity, a body would need to travel at 37 miles per second (59.5 km per second)—the highest "escape velocity" needed on any planet. Earth's escape velocity is 7 miles per second (11.2 km per second).

## Longest storm
**First observed in 1665**, the Great Red Spot is a massive storm that is still raging today. Winds blast an area 1.3 times as wide as Earth's diameter at speeds of up to 400 mph (644 km/h).

## Most massive
Being the biggest, it's no surprise that Jupiter is also the planet with the most mass, weighing in at a huge 4,184,000,000,000,000,000,000,000,000 lb (1,898,000,000,000,000,000,000,000,000 kg). This planetary powerhouse is 318 times more massive than Earth.

Spots visible on the surface of Jupiter are terrific storms resulting from the planet's fast spin and strong winds.

Brown and white striped bands are swirling gas clouds caused by Jupiter's speedy spin.

**MAGNETS** WOULD WORK WELL ON JUPITER, WHERE THE MAGNETIC FIELD IS 14 TIMES STRONGER THAN ON EARTH.

IT TAKES JUPITER 12 EARTH YEARS TO ORBIT THE SUN. IN ASTRONOMY THIS IS CALLED A "JOVIAN YEAR."

# THE OUTER PLANETS

The three planets farthest from the sun are **Saturn**, **Uranus**, and **Neptune**. Like Jupiter, they are known as **gas giants**.

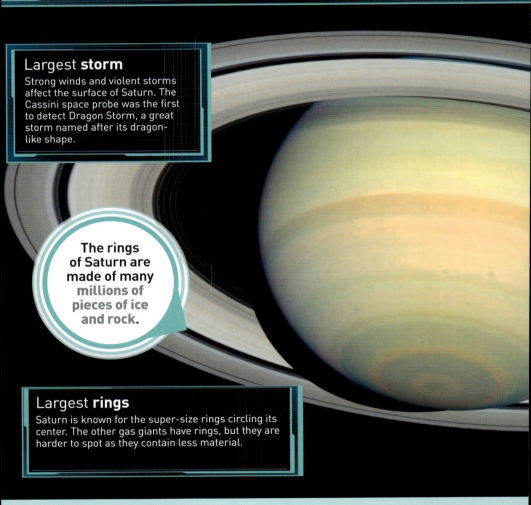

### Largest **storm**
Strong winds and violent storms affect the surface of Saturn. The Cassini space probe was the first to detect Dragon Storm, a great storm named after its dragon-like shape.

The rings of Saturn are made of many **millions of pieces of ice and rock**.

### Largest **rings**
Saturn is known for the super-size rings circling its center. The other gas giants have rings, but they are harder to spot as they contain less material.

SATURN IS NAMED AFTER THE ROMAN GOD OF TIME AND AGRICULTURE. HE WAS ALSO THE FATHER OF JUPITER.

IN GREEK MYTHOLOGY, URANUS WAS THE FIRST GOD AND THE DEITY FROM WHOM ALL THE OTHER GODS AND GODDESSES WERE DESCENDED.

**Saturn, Uranus, and Neptune** are made mainly of helium and hydrogen gas with a small rocky core. Saturn is the second-biggest planet in the solar system. Neptune is the smallest gas giant but is still nearly four times bigger than Earth.

## FAST FACTS

**The coldest planets** are Uranus and Neptune. Methane gas makes them both look blue.

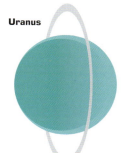
Uranus

**Most rings** Uranus has the most rings of any planet, but they are too faint to see.

**Only planet to rotate on its side** The other planets spin upright, but Uranus was knocked on to its side.

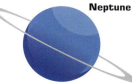
Neptune

**Coldest planet** Chilly Neptune has an average temperature of −353°F (−214°C).

**Strongest winds** Neptune has the fastest winds, blowing up to 1,300 mph (2,100 km/h).

## Strongest **lightning**
The most powerful lightning strikes occur on Saturn in an area called Storm Alley. The Cassini probe has captured these fabulous flashes on camera.

## Least dense planet
Saturn is the least dense of all the planets in the solar system. As a result, if Saturn was dropped into water, it would actually float!

**THE BLUE COLOR OF NEPTUNE IS WHY THE PLANET SHARES ITS NAME WITH THE ROMAN GOD OF THE SEA.**

**1781**
**URANUS WAS DISCOVERED IN 1781 BY THE GERMAN BRITISH ASTRONOMER WILLIAM HERSCHEL.**

ASTRONOMER GALILEO GALILEI FIRST OBSERVED JUPITER'S MOONS IN 1610.

# MOONING AROUND

A **moon** is a **"natural satellite"**—an object that **orbits** a planet or asteroid. There are **219 known moons** orbiting the **planets** of the solar system.

**Smoothest moon**
Europa is an icy moon with barely any craters. With the exception of a few ridges just a few hundred yards (meters) high, its surface is virtually flat.

*Europa*

*Ganymede*

**Most volcanic activity**
Io, Jupiter's third-largest moon, is covered in active volcanoes spewing sulfur into space. Many planets and moons have evidence of past volcanoes, but apart from Earth, the only places with known active volcanoes are moons (Io, Neptune's Triton, and Saturn's Enceladus).

*Io*

*Dactyl*

**First asteroid moon**
Discovered by the *Galileo* spacecraft in 1994 orbiting the asteroid 243 Ida, Dactyl proved the theory that asteroids could have their own moons.

**Dactyl** is just **1 mile (1.4 km)** in diameter. It orbits **40 miles (65 km)** from **243 Ida**.

**TITAN, ORBITING SATURN, IS THE ONLY MOON (AFTER OUR MOON) WHERE A SPACECRAFT HAS LANDED.**

**SATURN HAS 146 MOONS. TITAN, THE LARGEST, IS AS BIG AS MERCURY; THE SMALLEST ARE THE SIZE OF BOULDERS.**

CALLISTO, EUROPA, AND GANYMEDE ARE ICY, BUT IO IS VOLCANIC. 159

Callisto

**Most craters**
Callisto, Jupiter's second-largest moon (and the third-largest in the solar system), is the most heavily cratered object in the solar system.

**Biggest moon**
Ganymede, one of Jupiter's possible 92 moons, is 3,270 miles (5,262 km) in diameter. That's bigger than the planet Mercury.

## FAST FACTS

**These are the biggest moons** in the solar system relative to the bodies they orbit. The measurements are diameters.

**Biggest relative to a planet**

Earth — 7,917.5 miles (12,742 km)

The moon — 2,159 miles (3,474 km)

= 27 percent of Earth's size

**Biggest relative to a dwarf planet**

Pluto — 1,477 miles (2,377 km)

Charon — 753 miles (1,212 km)

= 51 percent of Pluto's size

**Relatively biggest of all**

Asteroid 69230 Hermes — 0.37 miles (0.6 km)

Its moon — 0.33 miles (0.54 km)

= 90 percent of Hermes's size

**Jupiter has the most moons**—to date, 92 moons have been identified orbiting the planet. (There are 55 known and named, and another 37 to be confirmed.) Four of them—Io, Europa, Ganymede, and Callisto—were the first moons after Earth's moon to be discovered, back in 1610.

**FIVE OF NEPTUNE'S 16 MOONS, INCLUDING TRITON, ORBIT IN THE OPPOSITE DIRECTION TO ITS 11 OTHER MOONS.**

**BECAUSE OF THE WAY IT TILTS AND ITS WIDE ORBIT AROUND THE SUN, WINTER IN URANUS LASTS FOR 21 LONG, CHILLY YEARS!**

**ASTEROIDS ARE THE BITS LEFT OVER WHEN PLANETS FORMED 4.6 BILLION YEARS AGO.**

### INTERSTELLAR VISITOR

**In 2017**, astronomers discovered an asteroid approaching the sun on a strange orbit that was eventually confirmed to come from beyond the solar system. Named Oumuamua, this strange elongated rock is 1,300 ft (400 m) long, and the first interstellar asteroid ever to be identified.

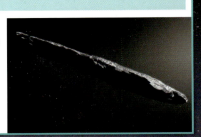

**Longest comet tail**
Comet Hyakutake has the longest measured tail at 354 million miles (570 million km). It could reach from the sun to beyond the asteroid belt between Mars and Jupiter!

**Most disruptive comet**
The tail of comet McNaught created such a large disturbance in the solar wind that the probe Ulysses took 18 days to travel through it. By contrast, Ulysses crossed the disturbance created by Hyakutake in just 2.5 days.

> Despite its brightness, the **comet's rocky core** is thought to be as black as coal!

**Biggest comet nucleus**
The nucleus (core) of comet Bernardinelli-Bernstein is estimated to be at least 80 miles (129 km) wide, about 50 times wider than the average comet.

Comets are "dirty snowballs" of snow and rock. Trillions of them lurk at the edge of the solar system, but we can only see and measure them when they fall toward the sun. Then, as a comet's solid nucleus warms up, the comet develops a planet-size atmosphere called a coma, which often has long tails of gas and dust streaming behind it in the solar wind of particles blowing out from the sun.

WHEN ASTEROIDS FALL TO EARTH, THEY BECOME KNOWN AS METEORITES. AROUND **17** OF THEM STRIKE THE EARTH EVERY DAY.

AROUND 90 PERCENT OF **ASTEROIDS** IN OUR SOLAR SYSTEM LIE IN THE "ASTEROID BELT" BETWEEN JUPITER AND MARS.

THERE ARE AROUND 1.9 MILLION ASTEROIDS IN OUR SOLAR SYSTEM.

**Fastest-spinning dwarf in space**
Haumea is an egg-shaped dwarf planet, which rotates end over end every four hours. Astronomers nicknamed Haumea "Santa," because it was discovered just after Christmas in 2004.

**Biggest belt object**
The largest body in the asteroid belt is Ceres. At 587 miles (945 km) wide, Ceres is a dwarf planet that is rocky and ringless, and has a very thin atmosphere.

**First dwarf planet**
Pluto was discovered in 1930 and with a diameter of 1,476 miles (2,376 km) used to be thought of as the ninth and smallest planet. However, it was reclassified as a dwarf planet in 2006.

# SPACE ROCKS

There is more to our solar system than planets and moons. **Comets, asteroids,** and **dwarf planets** can all be spotted whizzing around space.

 ABOUT 1 MILLION "SHOOTING STARS" ARE VISIBLE EVERY DAY. MOST ARE JUST SMALL ROCKS AND SPACE DUST.

**170** EARTH IS SCARRED BY MORE THAN 170 CRATERS WHERE LARGE METEORS HAVE HIT THE SURFACE.

### FIRST MOON WALK

**On July 21, 1969,** as part of the Apollo 11 mission, Neil Armstrong and Buzz Aldrin became the first humans to walk on the moon. This is a picture Armstrong took of Aldrin—his reflection is clearly visible in the visor of Aldrin's space helmet. The pair spent around two and a quarter hours on the lunar surface.

THE SPACE SHUTTLE'S FLIGHT DECK HAS MORE THAN 2,020 DIALS AND DISPLAYS.

# ROCKETING AHEAD

From **satellites** to **shuttles**, people have sent a lot of **high-tech hardware** into space. But which was the **first** or the **fastest**, and which traveled the **farthest**?

**First artificial satellite**
The basketball-size Russian satellite *Sputnik 1* broadcast radio signals from low Earth orbit for 21 days in 1957.

**First manned spacecraft**
Spending 108 minutes in space in April 1961, *Vostok 1* made one orbit of Earth with Soviet cosmonaut Yuri Gagarin on board.

**Fastest launch speed**
In 2006, the *New Horizons* probe, designed to fly by Pluto, made the fastest launch, with speeds of 36,373 mph (58,536 km/h)—that's more than 9.9 miles (16 km) per second.

**First rocket in space**
Designed as a weapon during World War II, a German V-2 missile reached an altitude of 109 miles (176 km) during a test launch in 1944.

**55** *VOYAGER 1* AND *2* BOTH CONTAIN GREETINGS RECORDED IN 55 LANGUAGES IN CASE THEY MEET ALIENS ON THEIR TRAVELS.

WHEN IT LAUNCHES IN 2025, THE **SPACEX STARSHIP** AT 397 FT (121 M) WILL BE THE TALLEST ROCKET TO GO INTO SPACE.

2022 WAS A RECORD-BREAKING YEAR, WITH 180 SUCCESSFUL ROCKET LAUNCHES.

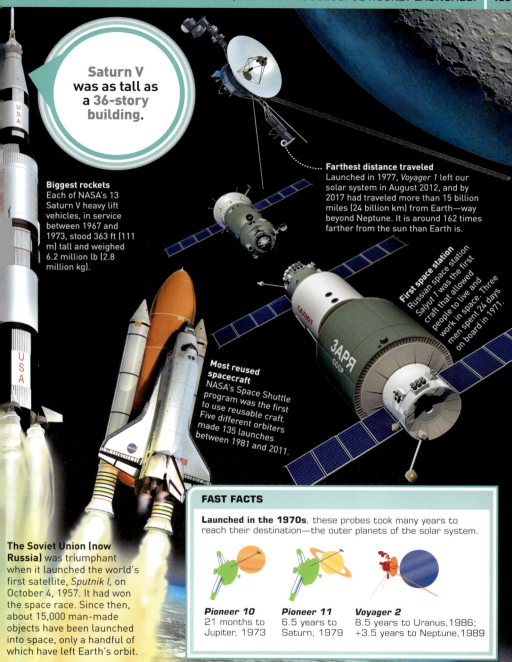

**Saturn V was as tall as a 36-story building.**

**Biggest rockets**
Each of NASA's 13 Saturn V heavy lift vehicles, in service between 1967 and 1973, stood 363 ft (111 m) tall and weighed 6.2 million lb (2.8 million kg).

**Farthest distance traveled**
Launched in 1977, *Voyager 1* left our solar system in August 2012, and by 2017 had traveled more than 15 billion miles (24 billion km) from Earth—way beyond Neptune. It is around 162 times farther from the sun than Earth is.

**First space station**
Russian space station *Salyut 1* was the first craft that allowed people to live and work in space. Three men spent 24 days on board in 1971.

**Most reused spacecraft**
NASA's Space Shuttle program was the first to use reusable craft. Five different orbiters made 135 launches between 1981 and 2011.

**The Soviet Union (now Russia)** was triumphant when it launched the world's first satellite, *Sputnik I*, on October 4, 1957. It had won the space race. Since then, about 15,000 man-made objects have been launched into space, only a handful of which have left Earth's orbit.

### FAST FACTS

**Launched in the 1970s,** these probes took many years to reach their destination—the outer planets of the solar system.

**Pioneer 10**
21 months to Jupiter, 1973

**Pioneer 11**
6.5 years to Saturn, 1979

**Voyager 2**
8.5 years to Uranus, 1986; +3.5 years to Neptune, 1989

**SOVIET COSMONAUT VALENTINA TERESHKOVA BECAME THE FIRST WOMAN IN SPACE IN 1963.**

**IN EARLY 2007, THE *NEW HORIZONS* PROBE USED JUPITER'S GRAVITY TO SLINGSHOT ITSELF FARTHER—AND FASTER—INTO OUTER SPACE!**

THE ISS ORBITS 250 MILES (400 KM) ABOVE EARTH.

# SENSATIONAL SPACE STATION

Since **1998**, the International Space Station (**ISS**) and the **astronauts** aboard it have been **breaking** a number of **records** in space.

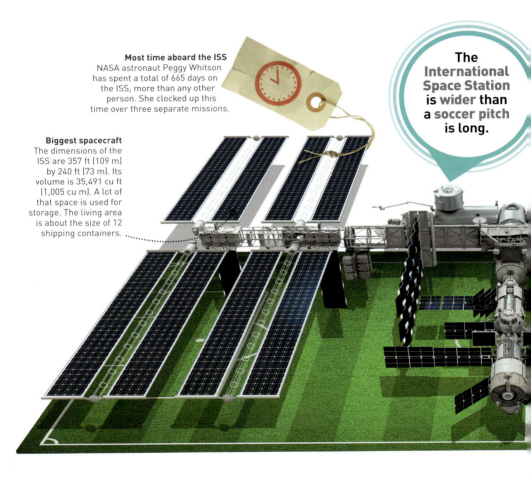

**Most time aboard the ISS**
NASA astronaut Peggy Whitson has spent a total of 665 days on the ISS, more than any other person. She clocked up this time over three separate missions.

**Biggest spacecraft**
The dimensions of the ISS are 357 ft (109 m) by 240 ft (73 m). Its volume is 35,491 cu ft (1,005 cu m). A lot of that space is used for storage. The living area is about the size of 12 shipping containers.

The **International Space Station** is **wider** than a **soccer pitch** is long.

 THE ISS TRAVELS IN SPACE AT 17,500 MPH (28,000 KM/H) AND COMPLETES ONE ORBIT OF **EARTH** EVERY 90 MINUTES.

 IN 2022–2023, US ASTRONAUT FRANK RUBIO LIVED ON THE ISS FOR 371 DAYS— THE LONGEST STAY ON THE VESSEL.

**ASTRONAUTS HAVE CARRIED OUT MORE THAN 260 SPACEWALKS FROM THE ISS.**

The first section, or module, of the ISS was launched in November 1998. Two years later, the first astronauts were able to live and work on board. After adding more modules, including science labs, solar arrays, and robotic arms, the building was finished in 2011. But work began again in 2016, with plans to send more modules over the next few years.

### FAST FACTS

**The first space station**, *Salyut 1*, was launched by the Soviet Union (now Russia), in 1971. Not only much smaller than the ISS, it also spent less time in space: just 175 days. It made 2,929 orbits of Earth, before it was intentionally destroyed.

**Length**: 65 ft (20 m)
**Width**: 13 ft (4 m)
**Volume**: 3,500 cu ft (99 cu m)

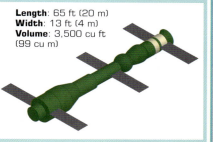

**Heaviest spacecraft**
Including all the modules up to 2011, the ISS weighs 925,335 lb (419,725 kg)—three times as much as *Mir*, which was the next-largest and heaviest space station. The ISS's weight is equivalent to that of 320 cars.

**Longest continuously inhabited spacecraft**
There have been astronauts at the ISS since November 2000, with new crews coming out to replace returnees. It broke the record for the longest continuously inhabited spacecraft back in 2010, when it beat *Mir's* 3,644 days.

**Most science in space**
In March 2017, the six-person crew of Expedition 50—made up of one European (ESA) and two NASA astronauts and three Russian cosmonauts—achieved 99 hours of scientific research on the ISS in one week.

**Most expensive object ever**
With a price tag as high as $150 billion (£120 billion), the ISS is not just the most expensive spacecraft but also the costliest item ever built, both on Earth and in space.

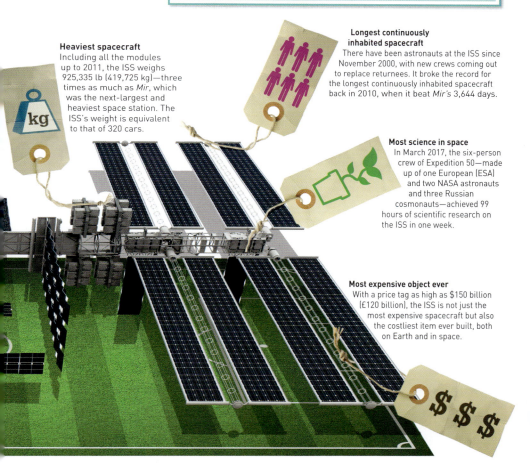

IN 2001, PIZZA HUT PERSUADED RUSSIAN COSMONAUTS TO TAKE A **PIZZA** TO THE ISS. IT WAS THE FIRST FAST-FOOD DELIVERY IN SPACE!

ASTRONAUTS USE **SLEEPING BAGS** ON THE ISS. THEY ARE TIED DOWN TO STOP THEM FLOATING OFF IN ZERO GRAVITY.

**IN 2019, FAST RECEIVED SIGNALS FROM A GALAXY 3 BILLION LIGHT-YEARS AWAY ...**

### GIANT TELESCOPE

**The world's biggest optical telescope** is Gran Telescopio Canarias (GTC) in Tenerife, Canary Islands, Spain. It has a 34 ft (10.4 m) wide aperture (opening) and 36 mirrored panels to focus visible light from space.

During its trial run **FAST** detected **two pulsars** (spinning neutron stars).

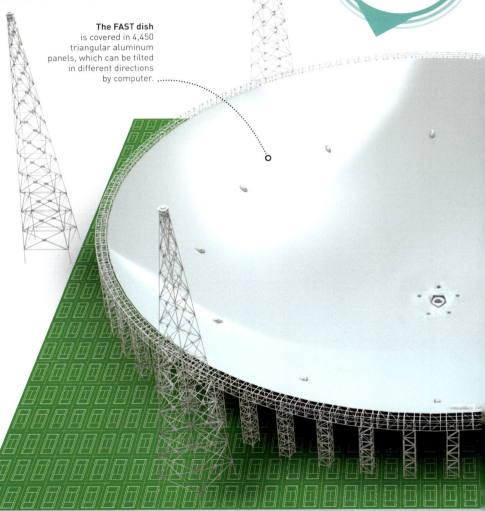

**The FAST dish** is covered in 4,450 triangular aluminum panels, which can be tilted in different directions by computer.

FAST WAS BUILT IN A REMOTE AREA TO REDUCE INTERFERENCE BY RADIO WAVES FROM **CELL PHONES** IN TOWNS AND CITIES.

FAST DETECTED THE BIGGEST **ATOMIC CLOUD** EVER IN 2022. IT WAS 20 TIMES BIGGER THAN OUR MILKY WAY GALAXY.

... THEY ARE CALLED FAST RADIO BURSTS (FRB) AND THEIR ORIGINS ARE A MYSTERY.

# THE BIGGEST DISH

The **world's biggest telescope** is the Five-hundred-meter Aperture Spherical Telescope (**FAST**) in China. As the name suggests, the dish measures an incredible **500 m (1,640 ft)** across.

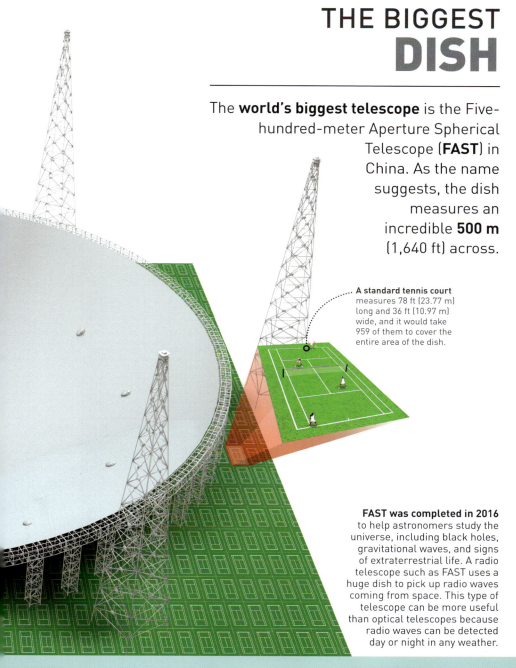

**A standard tennis court** measures 78 ft (23.77 m) long and 36 ft (10.97 m) wide, and it would take 959 of them to cover the entire area of the dish.

**FAST was completed in 2016** to help astronomers study the universe, including black holes, gravitational waves, and signs of extraterrestrial life. A radio telescope such as FAST uses a huge dish to pick up radio waves coming from space. This type of telescope can be more useful than optical telescopes because radio waves can be detected day or night in any weather.

 FAST HAS BECOME A **TOURISM** HOT SPOT SINCE OPENING. AROUND 2,000 PEOPLE VISIT THE TELESCOPE EACH WEEKEND.

 FAST HAS BEEN NICKNAMED *TIANYAN*, OR "THE HEAVENLY **EYE**," BY LOCALS BECAUSE OF ITS ABILITY TO "SEE" BACK TO THE DAWN OF TIME.

**SEATS ON PRIVATE SPACE FLIGHTS COST UP TO $500,000 (£398,000).**

# Space data

## BIG BUILD

The biggest thing in the universe is the **Hercules-Corona Borealis Great Wall**. It's not a physical wall, but a probable galaxy supercluster of stars. It is an average of **6–10 billion** light-years across and contains billions of galaxies.

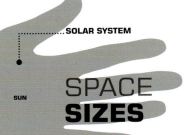

## SPACE SIZES

If the **SOLAR SYSTEM** could shrink to fit in the palm of your hand, **the SUN** would be smaller than **a grain of sand**. On the same scale, **the MILKY WAY** would be the **size of North America**.

## SPACE WALKS

**12 MINUTES**—DURATION OF FIRST SPACEWALK (ALEXEI LEONOV, 1965)

**8 HOURS, 56 MINUTES**—LONGEST SPACEWALK (JIM VOSS AND SUSAN HELMS, 2001). THAT'S MORE THAN **44 TIMES** LONGER.

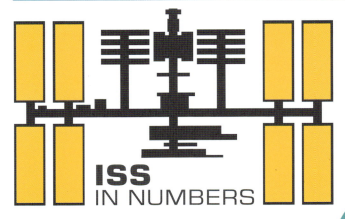

## ISS IN NUMBERS

**8 MILES** (12.9 KM) **OF ELECTRICAL WIRING** ON BOARD

**52 COMPUTERS** CONTROL THE **ISS SYSTEMS**

**42 FLIGHTS** TO BUILD **THE ISS**

**27,000 SQ FT** (2,500 SQ M) **OF SOLAR PANELS** PROVIDE POWER

IN 1950, US FARMERS PAUL AND EVELYN TRENT TOOK WHAT IS CLAIMED TO BE THE FIRST PHOTO OF AN **UNIDENTIFIED FLYING OBJECT** (UFO).

A 2008 EUROPEAN SPACE AGENCY ASTRONAUT JOB AD GOT MORE THAN **8,400 REPLIES**

# PLANETARY TIME

**MERCURY** HAS THE LONGEST DAY, EQUAL TO 176 EARTH DAYS.

**JUPITER** HAS THE SHORTEST DAY, **9 HOURS AND 56 MINUTES** LONG.

**NEPTUNE** HAS THE LONGEST YEAR, TAKING **164.8 EARTH YEARS** TO ORBIT ONCE AROUND THE SUN.

**MERCURY** HAS THE SHORTEST YEAR OF ALL THE PLANETS, **87.9 DAYS**.

# SPEED IN SPACE

THE FASTEST **A HUMAN** HAS EVER **TRAVELED IS** **24,791 mph (39,897 km/h)**

THIS WAS EXPERIENCED BY **THE CREW** OF **APOLLO** 10 ON THEIR WAY BACK TO **EARTH** FROM **ORBITING THE MOON** IN 1969.

## PASSPORT TO THE PLANETS

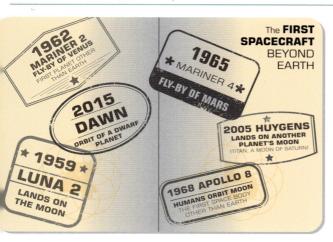

The **FIRST SPACECRAFT** BEYOND EARTH

- **1962 MARINER 2** FLY-BY OF VENUS, FIRST PLANET OTHER THAN EARTH
- **1965 MARINER 4** FLY-BY OF MARS
- **2015 DAWN** ORBIT OF A DWARF PLANET
- **2005 HUYGENS** LANDS ON ANOTHER PLANET'S MOON (TITAN, A MOON OF SATURN)
- **1959 LUNA 2** LANDS ON THE MOON
- **1968 APOLLO 8** HUMANS ORBIT MOON, THE FIRST SPACE BODY OTHER THAN EARTH

# MEMORABLE MOONS

**ENCELADUS** — The **MOST REFLECTIVE** body in space, reflecting more than **90 percent** of the energy it receives from **sunlight**.

**MIRANDA** — Home to the **BIGGEST CLIFF** in the **solar system**. Verona Rupes is thought to be **12.4 MILES (20 km)** tall.

**NESO** — The most **DISTANT MOON** from its planet, orbiting an average **30.8 million miles** (49.5 million km) from Neptune.

**PHOBOS** — The **CLOSEST MOON** to its planet, **3,700 miles (5,980 km)** above **MARS**— 66 **times closer** than our moon to Earth.

---

THE FIRST PRIVATELY FUNDED "SPACE TOURISM" TRIP INTO SPACE WAS BY **SPACESHIPONE** IN 2004.

THE **SUN** IS HALFWAY THROUGH ITS LIFE AND WILL CONTINUE TO SHINE FOR ANOTHER FIVE BILLION YEARS.

# INDEX

100-meter race 51, 66–7, 68, 71, 104
243 Ida 158

## A

adventurers 38–9
Africa
 deserts 20–1
Airbus A380 86, 87
aircraft 80–1, 86–9
airships 42, 86–7
Akers, Michelle 55
albatrosses
 Laysan 125
 wandering 107
Aldrin, Buzz 146–7, 163
amphibians 126
Amundsen, Roald 42, 44
anaconda, green 117
Angel Falls (Venezuela) 28
animals 100–35
 babies 122–3
 deadliest 127
 life spans 124–5
 migrations 110–1
 physical characteristics 102–3
 speed 104–5
Antarctic Plateau 45
Antarctica
 deserts 9, 21
 exploration 44–5
 ice cores 25
 lakes 29
 temperatures 9
Antonov An-225 86
ants, stings 115
apes 120–1
Apollo missions 147, 163, 171
Arabian Desert 20, 22–3
*Arabidopsis* 144
Aral Sea 26, 27
*El Arbol del Tule* 137
*Archaefructus* 139
Arctic exploration 42–3
Arctic Ocean 26, 27
Arctic terns 110–1
*Argentinosaurus* 128
armadillos, giant 127
Armstrong, Neil 146–7, 162–3
Ashford, Evelyn 67

Asia
 deserts 20, 22–3
 lakes 29
 population 11
asteroid belt 160
asteroids 8, 158–9, 160–1
astronauts 162–3, 166–7, 170–1
Atacama Desert (Chile) 20
athletics 50–1, 62–71
Atlantic Ocean 26, 27, 28, 29, 38, 42
*Aurornis xui* 132
Australia 11, 17, 38, 39, 47
*Avengers: Endgame* 34

## B

babies, mammal 122–3
Bågenholm, Anna 46
Bagger 293 Bucket Excavator 92–3
Baikal, Lake (Russia) 28
Balchen, Bernt 45
bananas 142
Bancroft, Ann 45
Bandaranaike, Sirimavo 33
Bangladesh 18
Barényi, Béla 92
Barton, Otis 38
baseball 56–7
basketball 61
Baumgartner, Felix 39
Beamon, Bob 62, 63
Beebe, William 38
bees, carpenter 103
beetles, Hercules 114
Bell X-1 80–1
Bellingshausen, Admiral Fabian 44
*Ben Hur* 35
Benz, Karl 76
The Bible 37
Bican, Josef 52
"Big Boy" 79
Binder, Brad 59
Bingham Canyon mine (US) 24–5
birds 105, 106–11
Bloodhound 82
Boeing 747 80–1
Bogucki, Robert 47
Bolt, Usain 51, 66, 67, 68–9, 71
Bonds, Barry 57
books 36–7
boomerang nebula 149

Brazil
 soccer team 48–9, 50, 53, 55
Breguet brothers 80
Bruce, Charles G. 41
budgerigars 108–9
buildings 96–9
Bumble Bee II 86–87
Burj Khalifa (Dubai) 28, 74–5, 96, 97
burrows 118–9
butterflies 100–1
Byrd, Richard 45

## C

cacti 138, 141, 144
Cafu 48–9
Cairo (Egypt) 10, 96
Callisto 159
Canada 19, 38, 136
canyons 150, 151
cap fungus 145
capybaras 118, 119
carats 17
caribou 110
cars 76–7
 land-speed 82–3
 motor racing 58–9
Cassini probe 156, 157
Castro, Fidel 33
Cayley, George 80
Ceni, Rogério 53
Ceres 161
Challenger Deep 39
Channel Tunnel (England–France) 98
Charon 159
cheetahs 104, 105
Cherrapunji (India) 9
Chichester, Francis 39
Chile 8, 15, 20, 47
chimpanzees 120
China
 books 36, 37
 buildings 98, 99
 Great Wall 94–5
 population 11, 13
 telescope 168–9
Christie, Agatha 36, 37
Christyakova, Galina 63
Chrysler Building (New York) 96
cities
 population 10–1
 Shanghai 12–3
climate 9, 29
coco de mer seeds 143
Codex Sassoon 37
Comăneci, Nadia 72–3
comets 160–1

comics 37
Connolly, James 50
copper 24
cosmonauts 144, 167
Crawler Transporter (NASA) 92
Crocker, Betty 36
crocodiles, saltwater 102
Cugnot, Nicolas-Joseph 77
Curiosity rover 152–3
cyclones, tropical 29
cypresses, Montezuma 137

## D

Dactyl 158
Daimler, Gottlieb 76
Dallol (Ethiopia) 9
Danilova, Elena 55
dark matter 148
Daulatpur-Saturia tornado 18
Dawn space probe 171
Delaware Aqueduct (US) 98
*Dendrobium appendiculatum* 138
Denmark Cataract 28
deserts 20–3, 47
Dhaka 11
Di Maggio, Joe 57
diamonds 16, 17
dinosaurs 128–31, 132, 134–5
*Diplodocus* 128, 130–1
Dolma, Dicky 41
dolphins 104, 113
*Don Quixote* 37
dragonflies, skimmer 110
Dubai 74–5, 96, 97, 99
dwarf planets 159, 161, 171

## E

Earhart, Amelia 38
Earth 6–29, 150–1, 159
earthquakes 8
eels, electric 127
eggs
 birds 106
 dinosaurs 131
El Reno tornado 19
electric cars 77
elephant creeper 141
elephants 104, 123
 African 103, 133
 Asian 124–5, 133

# INDEX

Elizabeth II, Queen 32
Elliott, Bill 59
Empire State Building (New York) 24, 25, 97
empress trees 137
Enceladus 158, 171
engineering 74–99
eruptions, volcanic 14–5
escape velocity 155
Europa 158, 159
Europe
  lakes 29
  population 11
Eustace, Alan 39
Everest, Mount 25, 27, 31–2, 40–1
extraterrestrial life 169
eyes, biggest 103

F

fangs, longest 117
FAST (Five-hundred-meter Aperture Spherical Telescope) 168–9
Finnbogadóttir, Vigdis 33
fish 103, 105, 111, 112–3, 132
flamingos 107
flight
  air pioneers 38, 80–1
  over Everest 41
  over Poles 42, 45
Flocken, Andreas 77
flowers 138–9, 144
flying boats 86
*Flying Scotsman* 79
*Fomitiporia ellipsoidea* 145
Fontaine, Just 52
food, survival without 46
football 61
*Formiga* 55
Formula One 58
fossils 130–1, 134–5, 139
Foyt, A.J. 58
froghoppers, common 115
fruit 142–3
Fuchs, Vivian 45
fungi 145

G

Gaet'ale Pond (Ethiopia) 28
galaxies 148, 149, 170

gamma rays 148
*Gandhi* 35
Ganymede 158–9
gas giants 154–7
gemstones 16–7
gibbons 120
giraffes 122
gliders 80, 87
goals 52–5
Gobekli Tepe (Türkiye) 95
gold
  medals 51
  mines 24, 25
  nuggets 17
*Gone with the Wind* 35
gorillas, Eastern 120
Gotthard Base Tunnel (Switzerland) 98–9
Gran Telescopio Canarias (GTC) 168
Grand Mosque of Djenne (Mali) 168
gravity 144
Great Pyramid of Giza (Egypt) 96
Great Sandy Desert (Australia) 47
Great Wall of China 94–5
Green, Andy 82–3
Greene, Maurice 67
Greenland 10
Gretzky, Wayne 61
Griffith-Joyner, Florence 67, 71
Gulf Stream 29
gymnastics 50, 72–3

H

Hadrian's Wall (UK) 94
hadrosaurs 131
Hamm, Mia 54
Harrison, William Henry 32
hat thrower fungus 145
Haumea 161
HD 100546 b 148
Heinkel He 178 V1 81
helicopters 80, 87
Helms, Susan 170
Helten, Inge 66
Hermes (asteroid 69230) 159
hibernation 126
Hillary, Sir Edmund 40, 45
Hindenburg LZ 129 86–9
Hines, Jim 67
Hoadley, David 18

honey fungus 145
hot-air balloons 80
Hughes H-4 Hercules 86
Humm, Fabienne 55
hummingbirds 106
humongous fungus 145
Hurst, Geoff 52
Huygens lander 171
Hyakutake comet 160
Hyperion 136

I

Ibuki, Mount (Japan) 9
IC 1101 galaxy 149
ice cores 25
ice hockey 61
India
  climate 9
  films 35
  forts 95
  population 11
Indian Ocean 26, 27, 29
Indonesia 11, 14, 15
Indycar 58, 59
insects 103, 110, 114–5, 124
International Space Station (ISS) 166–7, 170
invertebrates 126
Io 158,159
Isinbayeva, Yelena 64, 65, 70
Istanbul (Türkiye) 11

J

Jackson, Marjorie 66
Japan 9, 15, 32, 46
Java Trench 27
*Jaws* 34
Jbarah, Maysa 55
Jeddah Tower (Saudi Arabia) 96, 97
jellyfish, lion's mane 112
Jenatzy, Camille 77
jerboas
  long-eared 119
  pygmy 119
Jericho (Israel) 95
Johnson, Amy 38
Johnson, Walter 56
Jornet, Kilian 41
*Josephoartigasia monesi* 119
Jukichi, Oguri 46, 47
jumbo jets 80–1
June, Harold 45

Jupiter 148, 150, 154–5, 158, 159, 160, 165, 170
*Juramaia* 133

K

kangaroo rats 119
kangaroos 122
Kanneganti, Brahmanandam 35
King, Tom 52
Klose, Miroslav 52
koi carp 124
Kola Superdeep Borehole (Russia) 25
Krakatoa 14

L

Laerdal Tunnel (Norway) 98
lakes 6–7, 28–9
land-speed record 82–3
Large Hadron Collider 90–1, 149
Latynina, Larisa 50
lava 15
Lavillenie, Renaud 64
leaves 140–1
Leonov, Alexei 170
Lewis, Carl 67
Lhakpa Sherpa 40
life
  on Earth 151
  extraterrestrial 169
life spans 124–5
lightning 6–7, 157
Lincoln Cathedral (UK) 96
Lindbergh, Charles 38, 81
Litke Deep 27
Lloyd, Carli 54
long jump 62–3, 70
*Lord of the Rings: The Return of the King* 35
Louis XIX of France 32
The Louvre (Paris) 98
Lumière brothers 34
*Luna 2* 171
Luyendyk, Arie 59

M

McGwire, Mark 57
machines 90–3
McIntyre, David 41
McKinley, Ashley 45
McMurdo Dry Valleys (Antarctica) 9
McNaught comet 160

# INDEX

Malakhov, Misha 43
malaria 127
*Mallard* 79
mamba, black 117
*Mamenchisaurus* 129
mammals
  babies 122–3
  prehistoric 133
  smallest 126
mammoths 133
Maracaibo, Lake
  (Venezuela) 6–7
Marcus, Siegfried 76
Mariana Trench 9, 25, 27, 39
*Mariner* spacecraft 171
marmosets, pygmy 121
Mars 150, 151, 152–3, 171
marsupials 122
Maybach, Wilhelm 76
Megalodon 132
*Megalosaurus* 131
Mercury 150–1, 171
Messerschmitt ME 321 87
Messi, Lionel 52
Messier 33 galaxy 148
Mexico City (Mexico) 10
migrations 101, 110–1
Mil Mi-26 87
Milky Way 170
mines 24–5, 47
*Mir* space station 167
Miranda 171
Miura, Yuichiro 41
MLB (Major League Baseball) 56–7
monarch butterflies 100–1
monarchs 32–3
monkeys 120–1
  howler 121
  proboscis 121
Montgolfier brothers 80
moon 159
  landings 146–7, 162–3
moons 158–9, 171
mosquitoes, anopheles 127
moths
  hawk 103
  Wallace's sphinx 115
MotoGP 58, 59
motorcycles 58–9, 76–7, 83
motorsport 58–9
mountaineers 30–1, 40–1
mountains 40, 151

movies 34–5
Mponeng gold mine (South Africa) 25

# N

naked mole-rats 125
Nakheel Tower (Dubai) 99
Namib Desert 21
Naruhito, Emperor 32
NASA X-43 81
NASCAR 58, 59
natural satellites 158–9
USS *Nautilus* 42, 43
Navy Curtiss NC-4 87
NBA (National Basketball Association) 61
nebulae 148, 149
Neptune 156–7, 165, 171
Neso 171
New Horizons probe 164
NFL (National Football League) 61
NGC 604 148
NHL (National Hockey League) 61
Nobile, Umberto 42
Norgay, Tenzing 40
North America lakes 29
North Polar Basin (Mars) 150, 151
North Pole 42–3
Northwest Passage 42
*Nyasasaurus parringtoni* 130
Nyiragongo, Mount (Republic of Congo) 15

# O

Oceania
  lakes 29
oceans 26–7, 42
  trenches 27
O'Connor, Peter 63
Oelsner, Marlies 67
Oklahoma (US) 18, 19
Old St. Paul's Cathedral (London) 96
Olympic Games 50–1, 62–9, 72–3
Olympus Mons (Mars) 150–151
open-pit mines 24–5, 92–3
Operation Sunshine 42
orangutans 120, 123
orcas 133

orchids, Shenzhen Nongke 139
Ormond House 44
ornithomimids 131
Oscars 35
ostriches 105, 106, 128
Oumuamua 160
Owens, Jesse 63, 66

# P

Pacific Ocean 26–7
Palma, Emilio Marcos 45
paper buildings 99
*Paraceratherium* 133
Paralympics 51
parrots, gray 106
particle accelerators 90–1
*Patagotitan* 128, 135
pearls 16
Peary, Robert 42
*Pennantia baylisiana* 137
*Pentaceratops* 128
peregrine falcons 105
Petronas Towers (Kuala Lumpur) 97
Petty, Richard 58, 59
Phelps, Michael 50
Piccard, Jacques 39
*Pioneer* spacecraft 165
placental mammals 122
Plaisted, Ralph 42
planets 148, 150–7
  dwarf 159, 161
  time 17´
plants 136–45
Pluto 159, 161
poison
  fungi 145
  insect stings 115
  plants 141, 144
  snake bites 116–7
pole vault 64–5, 70
population 10–1
porcupines 119
porpoises 103
  Dall's 126
ports, container 13
Post, Wiley 81
Powell, Mike 62–3, 70
prairie dogs 118–9
prehistoric creatures 128–35
primates 120–1
prime ministers 32–3
pronghorns 105
Puerto Rico Trench 27
pumpkins, Atlantic Giant 142

*Puya raimondii* 139
pyramids 96
pythons
  reticulated 116
  royal 125

# Q

Qinghai–Tibet railway 84–5
*Quetzalcoatlus* 128–9

# R

rabbits 122
radio waves 169
*Rafflesia arnoldi* 138
railroads 78–79, 84–5, 98
rainfall 9, 29
Redgrave, Sir Steve 51
redwood trees 136
reptiles 116–7, 124–5, 126
Réunion Island 29
Richter, Annagret 66
Ring of Fire 15
rings, planetary 156, 15
Ripken Jr., Cal 56
road tunnels 98
Robinson, Rocky 83
*Rocket* 78–9
rockets 164–5
rocks, space 160–1
rocky planets 150–1
rodents 118–9
Romero, Jordan 30–1, 41
Roosevelt, Franklin D. 32
Rose, Pete 57
Rossi, Valentino 58
rotation, planets 155, 157
Rowling, J. K. 36
Rub' al Khali 20, 22–3
rulers 32–3
Russia
  lakes 29
  mines 25
  trees 136
  volcanoes 15
Ryan, Nolan 56

# S

Sagrada Família (Barcelona) 99
Sahara Desert 21
sailfish 105
sailors 39, 46
Sakyamuni Pagoda (Shanxi) 99

# INDEX

Salar de Uyuni
    (Bolivia) 8
Salenko, Oleg 52
salmon, Atlantic 111
*Salyut 1* space station
    144, 165, 167
San José mine
    (Chile) 47
Sao Paulo (Brazil) 10
sapphires 16
satellites 164–5
Saturn 156–7, 158, 165
Saturn V rockets 165
sauropods 131
Schmidt, Justin 115
Schumacher, Michael
    58
Scott, Robert F. 44
Sears Tower (Chicago)
    97
seas 28
Selkirk, Alexander 47
Shakespeare, William
    36
Shanghai 11, 12–3
sharks
    great white 102, 110,
        113
    Greenland 125
    prehistoric 132
    whale 113, 133
shrews, Eurasian
    pygmy 127
shrimps, peacock
    mantis 126
Siffredi, Marco 40
*Sinbad: Legend of the
    Seven Seas* 35
Sinclair, Christine 54
skydiving 39
skyscrapers 74–5,
    96–7, 99
sleep, animals 126
Smith, Calvin 67
snakes 116–7, 125
snow 9
snowboarding 40
Sobhuza II of Swaziland
    32
soccer 48–9, 52–5, 60
solar system 150–63,
    165, 170
South Africa 8, 17, 25,
    150
South America
    deserts 20
    lakes 29
South Pole 44–5
South Sandwich Trench
    27
Southern Ocean 26, 27

Soviet Union 165, 167
space 146–71
    plants in 144
    records 148–9
space probes 156, 157,
    164, 165, 171
Space Shuttle 165
space stations 144, 165,
    166–7
space telescopes 149
spacewalks 170
*Spirit of St. Louis* 81
sport 48–73
sprinters 66–7
*Sputnik 1* 164,165
squid, colossal 103
steam engines 77
steam trains 78–9
*Stegosaurus* 128
stick insects 114–5
stings 115
storms, space 155, 156,
    157
Strasbourg Cathedral
    (France) 96
Stromboli, Mount (Italy)
    14
*Struthiomimus* 131
Strutt, Edward Lisle 41
Sun 170
superclusters, star 170
supersonic speeds 39,
    80–1, 82
survivors 46–7
swifts, spine-tailed 105
Sydney (Australia) 11

# T

Tabei, Junko 40
Tambora (Indonesia) 14
telescopes 149, 168–9
temperatures
    body 46
    Earth 9, 20
    space 149, 150, 157
termite queens 125
TGV V150 84
Thai Paper House
    (Bangkok) 99
*Therizinosaurus* 129
Thompson, Archie 52
Thrust SSC 82–3
time, planetary 171
titan arums 139
*Titanic* 35
titanosaurs 135
Toba, Mount 15
tornadoes 18–9
tortoises, Aldabra giant
    124
trains 78–9, 84–5, 98

transatlantic flights 80,
    81
trees 136–7, 140–1,
    157, 158
Trevithick, Richard 77
*Troodon* 128
tunnels 98–9
Tupolev Tu-144 81
twisters 18–9
*Tyrannosaurus rex*
    134–5
Tyus, Wyomia 66

# U

undersea tunnels 98
Uranus 156, 157, 159,
    165
US
    mines 24–5
    Olympic Games 51
    presidents 32
    tornadoes 18, 19
    trees 136–7
    volcanoes 15

# V

V-2 missiles 164
Valdivia (Chile) 8
Valles Marineris (Mars)
    150, 151
Vatican City 10
Venezuela 6–7, 28
venom 116–7
Venus 150–1
*Victoria amazonica*
    140–1
Videkull, Lena 55
viper, Gaboon 116
volcanoes 14–5, 26,
    150, 151, 158
Voss, Jim 170
*Vostok 1* 164
Vostok Research
    Station
    (Antarctica) 9, 25
*Voyager* spacecraft 165
Vredefort crater
    (South Africa) 8, 150

walls 94–5

# W

Walsh, Don 39
Wambach, Abby 54
Warby, Ken 83
water 26–9
    aqueducts 98
    on Earth 151
water-speed record 83
waterfalls 28
weather 9, 18–9, 29

Weihenmayer, Erik 40
wetas, giant 115
whales
    blue 112–3, 123, 127
    bowhead 124
    gray 110
    humpback 110, 111
    sperm 127
Whitson, Peggy 166
Williams, Percy 66
Williams, Ted 57
Williams, Willie 66
winds 18–9
    planetary 155, 157
wings
    aircraft 87
    birds 107
    prehistoric creatures
        128–9
*Wolffia globosa* 139
women's soccer 54–5,
    60
Woolworth Building
    (New York) 96
World Cup 50–1, 52, 54,
    60
World Trade Center
    (New York) 97
Wright, Orville and
    Wilbur 80

# Y

Yangtze River 13
Yeager, Chuck 81
Young, Cy 56

# Z

Zorn, Trischa 51

# ACKNOWLEDGMENTS

**Dorling Kindersley would like to thank:** Derek Harvey, John Woodward, and Giles Sparrow for consultancy work; Andrea Mills for editorial assistance; Hazel Beynon and Katie John for proofreading; Helen Peters for the index and Tanvi Sahu and Prateek Maurya for design assistance.

The publisher would like to thank the following for their kind permission to reproduce their photographs:

(Key: a-above; b-below/bottom; c-center; f-far; l-left; r-right; t-top)

**4 Alamy Stock Photo:** CNP Collection (crb); Xinhua (cla). **Depositphotos Inc:** CogentMarketing (crb/Frame). **Dreamstime.com:** Michael Drager (crb/Throne). **Getty Images:** Antonio Scorza / AFP (cra). **Rex by Shutterstock:** Sipa Press (ca). **5 Getty Images:** Anna Shtraus Photography (tl); Joel Sartore (tc). **NASA:** (tr); JPL / DLR (br). **6 Alamy Stock Photo:** Xinhua. **8 Dreamstime.com:** Dita Nemcova (c). **Getty Images / iStock:** dottedhippo (bl). **9 Alamy Stock Photo:** Jeffrey Miller (cb); Navapon Plodprong (cra). **Dreamstime.com:** Genadijs Zelenkovecs (cla). **Getty Images:** Subhendu Sarkar / LightRocket (ca). **Science Photo Library:** Sputnik (clb). **Shutterstock.com:** Granate Art (bl) **11 Getty Images:** Inkiad Hasin (tr). **Shutterstock.com:** ElenVD (bc). **12-13 Getty Images:** Ansonfina. **18-19 TurboSquid:** Alex_BY (cb); everlite (Rubble B). **18 Alamy Stock Photo:** Cultura Creative (RF) (clb). **19 TurboSquid:** 3degestar (cl). **20 Alamy Stock Photo:** Stephen Barnes (l). **Depositphotos Inc:** lkpro (r); Nyker (c). **Dreamstime.com:** Andreas Muth Hegener (br). **21 Alamy Stock Photo:** Juniors Bildarchiv GmbH (r). **Depositphotos Inc:** Goinyk (l). **22-23 Getty Images:** Buena Vista Images. **25 123RF.com:** Dmytro Nikitin (c). **Dreamstime.com:** Yehor Vlasenko (c). **26 Getty Images:** NASA / Earth Observatory / Handout / Corbis (clb). **27 Getty Images:** duncan1890 (bl). **30 Rex by Shutterstock:** Sipa Press. **32 Alamy Stock Photo:** CNP Collection (cra); Rodrigo Reyes Marin / ZUMA Wire (tl). **Getty Images:** Mark Cuthbert / UK Press (crb). **Depositphotos Inc:** CogentMarketing (Frame). **Dreamstime.com:** Michael Drager (Throne). **Getty Images:** Dubber / ullstein bild (c). **33 Alamy Stock Photo:** Icelandic photo agency (cr). **Depositphotos Inc:** Albund (Podium). **Getty Images:** Murali / Pix Inc. / The LIFE Images Collection (ca); Jorge Rey (cla). **34 Alamy Stock Photo:** Imaginechina Limited (c); Glasshouse Images (cb); Pictorial Press Ltd (cb). **34-35 Depositphotos Inc:** Mayakova (Popcorn); TitoOnz (Background). **35 Alamy Stock Photo:** AF archive (cl, c); Pictorial Press Ltd (cla); Photo 12 (ca); Robertharding (clb). **37 Alamy Stock Photo:** United Archives GmbH (bc). **38 Getty Images / iStock:** Lilkin (bl). **41 Getty Images:** Jeff Pachoud / AFP (tr). **123RF.com:** David Benes (bc). **42 Alamy Stock Photo:** Granger Historical Picture Archive (cl). **Getty Images:** Bettmann (clb); Mondadori Portfolio (cr); Universal History Archive / UIG (tr). **42-43 Alamy Stock Photo:** Antiqua Print Gallery. **Depositphotos Inc:** PicsFive (Background). **43 Getty Images:** Alexander Sentsov / ITAR-TASS (cb); US Navy / The LIFE Images Collection (c). **Shutterstock.com:** GelgelNasution (br). **44 Alamy Stock Photo:** Paul Fearn (cr); Interfoto (cb); Pavel Stasevich (bc). **Getty Images:** Bettmann (br). **Alamy Stock Photo:** Pavel Stasevich (bc). **44-45 Alamy Stock Photo:** Antiqua Print Gallery (Map). **Depositphotos Inc:** PicsFive (Background). **45 Getty Images:** Corbis (tl); Hulton-Deutsch Collection / Corbis (tr); Mark McDonald / MCT (crb). **46-47 Dreamstime.com:** Daniel Domański (Background); Feng Yu (Paper). **47 Alamy Stock Photo:** Chris Hellier (cr); WENN UK (cl). **Depositphotos Inc:** PicsFive (t); Stillfx (cr). **Dreamstime.com:** Axstokes (br); Photka. **48 Getty Images:** Antonio Scorza / AFP. **50 Getty Images:** Everett Collection Historical (ca). **Dreamstime.com:** Terriana (bc). **52 Alamy Stock Photo:** Action Plus Sports Images (cra). **52-53 Alamy Stock Photo:** PA Images (all red jersey images). **54 Dreamstime.com:** Agung Santhani (bc). **55 Alamy Stock Photo:** Aflo Co., Ltd. (bc). **56-57 TurboSquid:** onurozgen. **57 Getty Images:** Bettmann (br). **58 Getty Images:** Vincenzo Pinto / AFP (clb) Mark Thompson (cla); Bettmann (ca); ISC Images & Archives (c). **62 Getty Images:** Bettmann (clb). **64 Getty Images:** Maja Hitij (clb). **65 Getty Images:** Ian Walton (cm). **67 Dreamstime.com:** Jerry Coli (cl). **Getty Images:** Bill Frakes / Sports Illustrated (c). **68-69 Getty Images:** Cameron Spencer. **72 Getty Images:** AFP (cra). **Shutterstock.com:** Fkdkondmi (bc). **72-73 Getty Images:** Vladimir Molnar (bl). **74 Getty Images:** Bettmann. **77 Getty Images:** Anna Shtraus Photography. **77 Getty Images:** Bettmann (cra). **79 Alamy Stock Photo:** Granger Historical Picture Archive (crb). **80 Dreamstime.com:** Mahmut Tibet (bl). **82 Alamy Stock Photo:** WENN Ltd (bl). **83 Science Photo Library:** Keith Kent (br). **84-85 Getty Images:** China Photos. **88 Getty Images:** Stocktrek Images (br). **88-89 Getty Images:** NY Daily News Archive. **90-91 Getty Images:** Richard Juilliart / AFP. **92 Alamy Stock Photo:** NASA Image Collection (clb). **92-93 Alamy Stock Photo:** Agencia Fotograficzna Caro. **94 Depositphotos Inc:** Sepavone (cb). **Dreamstime.com:** Martin Kemp / Martink (crb). **95 Depositphotos Inc:** Richie0703 (crb). **iStockphoto.com:** undefined undefined (cla); x-drew (cra). **Shutterstock.com:** Vladimir Molnar (bc). **97 Dreamstime.com:** Kseniia Sumkina (bc). **100 Getty Images:** Joel Sartore. **106 Alamy Stock Photo:** Svetlana Soloveva (bc). **108-109 FLPA:** Martin Willis / Minden Pictures. **110 Alamy Stock Photo:** Elizabeth Masoner (cla). **Dreamstime.com:** Aleksandr Mansurov (bl). **111 Dreamstime.com:** Vitaly Ilyasov (bc). **123 Getty Images:** Patrick Dykstra / Barcroft Images / Barcroft Media (ca). **124 Dorling Kindersley:** Jerry Young (bl). **Dreamstime.com:** Isselee (tr); Studioloco (c). **125 Alamy Stock Photo:** Sabena Jane Blackbird (bc). **Dorling Kindersley:** E.J. Peiker (c). **Dreamstime.com:** Werayut Nueathong (cr). **128 Dreamstime.com:** Svetlana Soloveva (bc). **130-131 Heyuan Dinosaur Museum. 133 Science Photo Library:** John Sibbick (clb). **134-135 Getty Images:** Mark Widhalm / Field Museum Library. **Getty Images:** Angela Weiss / AFP (c). **135 Dorling Kindersley:** Senckenberg Gesellschaft Fuer Naturforschung Museum (bl). **139 Dreamstime.com:** Andrey Yanushkov (bl). **141 Shutterstock.com:** ukmooney (bc). **146 NASA. 148 ESA / Hubble:** Hui Yang (University of Illinois) and NASA (cra); NASA (cb); NASA and the Hubble Heritage Team (STScI / AURA) (bc). **NASA:** ESO / L. Calçada (crb); Goddard Space Flight Center (clb). **148-149 Depositphotos Inc:** Colors06. **149 ESA / Hubble:** NASA and the Hubble Heritage Team (STScI / AURA) (fclb, cr/NGC 2174); NASA and The Hubble Heritage Team STScI / AURA (clb). **Getty Images:** Harald Ritsch / Science Photo Library (cl). **NASA:** ESA, Hubble Heritage Team (STScI / AURA) (cr); ESA, P. Oesch (Yale University), G. Brammer (STScI), P. van Dokkum (Yale University), and G. Illingworth (University of California, Santa Cruz) (crb). **150 NASA:** Johns Hopkins University Applied Physics Laboratory / Carnegie Institution of Washington (tl); JPL (c). **Dreamstime.com:** Elena Kozyreva (bc). **150-151 NASA:** NOAA / GOES Project (c). **151 NASA:** HQ (br). **Dreamstime.com:** Elena Kozyreva (bc). **152-153 NASA:** JPL-Caltech / MSSS. **154-155 NASA:** JPL-Caltech / SwRI / MSSS / Kevin M. Gill (b). **156-157 NASA:** ESA and Erich Karkoschka (University of Arizona) (c). **157 Shutterstock.com:** Lomakin (bl). **158-159 NASA:** JPL / DLR (cb). **158 NASA:** (cb); JPL / DLR (bl, c). **159 NASA:** JPL / DLR (German Aerospace Center) (tl). **160-161 NASA:** JHUAPL / SwRI (cb). **160 ESO:** (tc). **NASA:** (cb); European Southern Observatory (c); ESA / JPL-Caltech (ca); E. Slawik (b). **161 Alamy Stock Photo:** Science Photo Library (tr). **NASA:** JPL-Caltech / UCLA / MPS / DLR / IDA (crb). **162-163 NASA. 164 Alamy Stock Photo:** Trung Tran (b). **166-167 Alamy Stock Photo:** Nerthuz (cb). **Depositphotos Inc:** Andrey_Kuzmin (b). **Dreamstime.com:** Luminis (Tag). **168 Dreamstime.com:** Inge Hogenbijl (tl)

All other images © Dorling Kindersley Limited
For further information see: www.dkimages.com